OVERCOMING THE OVERCAST

OVERCOMING THE OVERCAST

NAVIGATING THE STORMS OF GRIEF WITH GOD

DR. AMANDA MCNEIL

Artwork by Andi Mejia-Travelute

In her book *Overcoming the Overcast: Navigating the Storms of Grief with God*, Dr. Amanda McNeil has crafted a captivating exploration of grief that transcends the traditional confines of mourning the loss of a loved one. This book is not just about death; it's about the myriad ways we encounter and navigate loss throughout our lives. Whether it's the death of a dream, the end of a relationship, or the loss of a sense of self, the author invites us into a deeply personal and universal journey.

JANIS SMITH, Ph.D., Master Life Coach, and President of Heritage University and Seminary

Loss is something you experience, and grief is something you process. Not everyone has the ability to process grief on their own. Many times, the pain is too deep. Dr. Amanda McNeil has a unique approach to grief, combining the spiritual and the practical so that the process flows the way it was meant to. I have experienced my share of loss in this life and Amanda's voice has been a critical part of the grieving process for me and my family. Her passion for people in this delicate stage of life is undeniable, and I am so thankful that God blessed me with the opportunity to have her in my corner during the most difficult times in my life.

ANTHONY CANAAN, MBA, business owner, and team pastor at City of Life Church

Amanda's book, shaped by her personal grief, steadfast faith, and pastoral expertise, offers hope and resonates with anyone facing loss. It feels like a comforting yet thought-provoking conversation with a wise friend and provides valuable guidance on the path to healing.

MARINA DURAN, pastor at Chel Church

While reading *Overcoming the Overcast*, I experienced the death of a close friend. I found myself immediately drawing from the things I had learned in its pages, both for myself and as I spoke to my friend's husband, who is now unexpectedly facing life without his partner of eleven years. Not only does Amanda write poignantly about her own grief journey, but she creates a strong and essential framework of theology surrounding God's character, His goodness, hope, and Heaven. This book is a compassionate and hope-filled resource for those struggling to make sense of life after loss.

CASSIE MORAIN, team pastor at City of Life Church

Dr. McNeil's book skillfully addresses the deep complementary relationship between psychology and Christian belief in her exploration of the universal human experience of grief. Sharing her personal journey and the observed experiences of others in processing life losses, she provides several lenses for consideration of the topic, including accessible knowledge from neuroscience and thoughtful consideration of Scripture. The eternal issues of life including God's identity, the meaning of life and death, and our origins and future as created beings in this world and beyond are addressed directly. Her writing does not present simple tidy explanations. Rather, she challenges her readers to thoughtfully process their own experiences with intentionality, while suggesting with hope that the grieving process has meaning as a gift from a good Father.

CLIFF HURNDON, Ph.D., FL Licensed Psychologist, qualified supervisor, and retired counselor educator

Amanda McNeil has counseled countless members of our congregation throughout her twelve years as a pastor on team at our church. Her professional qualifications for having a voice in the grief space are impressive but what sets her apart is her humility and willingness to continually share her own intimate experiences with grief throughout her lifetime.

AMY SMITH, senior pastor at City of Life Church

I wholeheartedly endorse Dr. Amanda McNeil as an exceptional licensed pastoral counselor with a specialization in grief. Her profound empathy and personal experience, including her journey of loss that inspired her insightful book, *Overcoming the Overcast: Navigating the Storms of Grief with God*, uniquely position her to guide individuals through their grief. Dr. McNeil skillfully helps those who are grieving find solace and strength by directing them back to God amidst their storm.

CHRISTOPHER SANCHEZ, Licensed Mental Health Counselor, A Second Wind Counseling

Losing my dad in 2021, was the most painful and traumatic experience of my life. During this dark time, Amanda was an extraordinary source of strength and wisdom. She walked and continues to walk alongside me through the depths of grief, providing both compassionate companionship and insightful counsel. Her ability to hold space for sorrow while gently guiding me forward is a rare gift. Amanda's friendship has been invaluable to me, and her voice is a powerful one that our world desperately needs. Her deep understanding of grief is beautifully articulated in this book, which is a testament to her wisdom and empathy. I am confident that her words will bring comfort, clarity, and hope to anyone navigating the complex journey of loss.

MARIELYS CANAAN, M.Ed., principal at City of Life Christian Academy, and team pastor at City of Life Church

Overcoming the Overcast is a beacon of hope for Christians grappling with loss. Combining her rich experience in church ministry with counseling wisdom, Amanda presents a heartfelt exploration of God's character and comfort during grief. Her insightful guidance offers readers a path to finding peace and strength.

TYLER GRAMLING, pastor at Potential Church

Amanda has continually been a voice of hope for me in seasons of "deepest darkness" (Psalm 23:4). Whether it's been encouragement from one of her sermons, a counseling session or a simple text message, Amanda's words have carried weight because I know they come from personal experience.

JESSICA REEDY, associate pastor at City of Life Church

Overcoming the Overcast is a personal and uplifting read. Amanda's brave sharing of her own journey and insights helps readers find hope and clarity through their own storms. Her blend of personal stories and biblical truths makes this a comforting guide for anyone seeking to see beyond their grief.

AMBER GRAMLING, pastor at Potential Church

For you, reader. May you overcome.

ACKNOWLEDGEMENTS

I am so grateful for the community who surrounded me and made this book possible.

Thank you to my Pastors, church family, colleagues, and clients for continually teaching me. I am regularly impacted by you and am honored to witness your stories. Thank you for contributing to my restoration.

Thank you to the professors who have poured into me over the years teaching from their education and experience to help me grow in my gifts and sharpen my skills in both understanding the Bible and counseling. Particularly, thank you to Professor Patti Cote, Dr. Clifford Hurndon, and Drs. Gary and Janis Smith for how you modeled integrating faith and psychology. I am eternally grateful for you.

Thank you to Dr. Timothy Jennings for all your work in the field, your thoughtful ministry, and your dialogues with me. This book is more precise because of your generosity.

Thank you to my editor, Abbey, for your patience and expertise to shine light and make such a murky message more clear.

Thank you to my consultant, Adam, for pouring into this book during the darkest storm of your life.

Thank you to my friend and marketing sage, Matt, for helping me look past the horizon and expand my vision for serving and impacting people through this book.

Thank you to my friend and designer, Andi, for making my ideas for the visuals of this book even better than I had them in my mind.

Thank you to my friend and assistant and layout designer and probably at least three other roles, Cassie, for pouring so much excellence and thought into this book. Witnessing how you have overcome storms of grief in your life is joyous for me and I treasure that we get to walk alongside each other in both the sunshine and rain.

Thank you to my group of friends who have prayed for me, checked in on the process, read snippets along the way, and have witnessed my journey of overcoming.

Thank you to my family for modeling how to keep walking forward amidst the storms of life.

Mom and Dad, thank you for planting the hope of eternity in my heart.

Malachi, thank you for bringing so much sunshine to my heart. Thank you for teaching me to celebrate and play in the rain. You are a profound gift.

Justin, thank you for being my lifelong hurricane party coordinator and partner in all we do. I cherish that you have been next to me for almost every storm of my life. Thank you for your support throughout my education and writing process - particularly the laundry and extra dada-son dates. And in all the overcast moments of my story thank you for your heart, your prayers, your stupid jokes just to make me laugh, and for facing your own storms along the way. You can stand under my umbrella.

CONTENTS

FOREWORD

Sometimes, we turn to nonfiction to expand our knowledge. Other times, we're searching for the answer to a question. No matter why you picked up *Overcoming the Overcast*, by the time you finish, you'll have found what you needed—and perhaps more.

I've known Dr. Amanda McNeil since she was a middle schooler in my church youth group in the 90s. As her pastor for over 25 years, I've seen her face personal tragedy and brokenness that could have led to a crisis of faith. Instead, she leaned into her faith, turning pain into a powerful catalyst for healing and redemption. Now, as both a pastoral and clinical counselor, she uses her experiences to help others. This book is excellent proof.

Jesus wept was always the answer to a Bible trivia question for me. As a pastor's kid, I was blessed in many ways, and grief often seemed like something other families went through. It wasn't until I was married with my first child that I truly experienced grief.

Our two-year-old daughter, Mia, began having trouble hearing. We took her for tests, and the short time between the tests and waiting for results changed everything. I had always trusted God in every area of my life, but this experience exposed a hidden fear: I had tied my happiness to the health and safety of my child. I hadn't realized how much I'd elevated that fear, believing that as long as my family was safe, everything else would be fine.

Grief forces us to confront what we hold dear. As a parent, the thought of losing a child is unbearable. And yet, there I was, helpless to change the situation. My faith was being tested in a way I had never imagined.

There's a story in Luke 8 about Jairus, a synagogue leader. His daughter was gravely ill, on the verge of death. In desperation, Jairus went to Jesus for help. But before they reached the house, a messenger came with devastating news: *"Your daughter is dead. Don't bother the teacher anymore."*

It's hard to imagine a more crushing moment. But Jesus turned to Jairus with words that must have seemed impossible to accept: *"Don't be afraid; just believe, and she will be healed."*

When they arrived at Jairus' house, Luke tells us Jesus only let Peter, John, James, and the girl's parents into the room. Sometimes, reading the Bible is like one of those illusions that says, *"I bet you didn't notice there was a mistake here."* You reread it, and it says, *"I bet bett you you didn't notice that that there was a mistake here here."* So annoying! Our eyes skip over what seems unimportant, and we miss crucial details.

Jesus was intentional about who entered the room. He knew not everyone could witness a miracle. Outside, professional mourners were already wailing, creating a dramatic display of grief that was common in Jewish customs. People replete with flutes and sad songs in minor keys were paid to cry at funerals, creating an atmosphere of discord and sadness. While there's a place for grief, this wasn't it—it was performative.

Jesus wasn't having any of it. *"Stop wailing,"* He told them. *"She's not dead but asleep."* And they laughed. Imagine that—moments earlier, they were wailing, and now they were laughing. You don't switch that easily unless your grief isn't real.

This contrast matters. Jesus wasn't just clearing the room of doubters; He was drawing a line between genuine grief and hopelessness. Sometimes, we have to do what Jesus did—clear out the noise and surround ourselves with people who make room for faith.

In the quiet, Jesus took the girl's hand, told her to get up, and her spirit returned. She stood up. In a beautifully human moment, Jesus told her parents to give her something to eat. I like to imagine He said, *"Give this girl some Oreos,"* though, of course, that's just my imagination. What He really said was, *"Give her something to eat,"* grounding the miraculous in the ordinary.

Her parents were astonished, I imagine in the most joyful, heart-bursting way possible. The professional mourners likely rationalized the miracle, claiming she hadn't been dead after all.

That's what faithless people do—they explain away miracles to avoid the deeper truth: God is sovereign, and some things only He can do, even when we don't understand.

While waiting for Mia's test results, I was surrounded by different voices. Some, though well-meaning, created an atmosphere of fear. I want to be clear: acknowledging the reality of a tough situation isn't a lack of faith, refusing to make room for the miraculous *is*. Thankfully, there were others who pointed me back to faith, reminding me that God was still present and in control. Like Jairus, I had to choose: would I listen to doubt, or would I trust Jesus?

Mia's hearing turned out fine. Today, she hears everything—except, of course, when I ask if she borrowed one of my missing Cowboys hoodies. I believe she experienced a miracle, but more than that, there was a miracle in me. Through that season, God showed me that grief isn't something we walk through alone. He is with us, asking us to trust Him, even when everything feels uncertain.

I've learned that grief doesn't come with easy answers. Sometimes, we don't get to know why certain things happen, or why we endure certain pains. But in those moments, I've found comfort in the shortest verse in the Bible: **Jesus wept**.

There's so much in those two words. Jesus, fully aware of the miracle He was about to perform, still entered into the grief around Him. He didn't rush past it. He sat in it. He wept. That moment in John 11:35 teaches us that God doesn't dismiss our suffering. He doesn't rush through it. He enters into it with us. He has a *plan for it*.

Hebrews 4:15 tells us that we have a High Priest who is not out of touch with our reality. He has experienced every aspect of humanity, including grief. Because of that, He can offer us comfort and peace in ways no one else can.

Jesus wept is still the answer to a Bible trivia question. But for me, it's become the answer to the deeper question of how to face grief when our hearts are broken.

JEFFREY SMITH, PHD.
Senior Pastor, City of Life Church
Author of *Jesus First, Jesus Always*

INTRODUCTION

The first time I remember experiencing loss, I was four years old. The first time I experienced loss that broke my heart, I was ten. Then again at thirteen. Then the hardest I've ever experienced at fourteen. And there's been several more since then.

Navigating life during loss can feel very similar to navigating during a storm. When life is dark and stormy, it is difficult to see and hear clearly. Our thinking can often be clouded, too. Our nervous system reaches higher alert as we grip the steering wheel or brace ourselves on an airplane experiencing turbulence. Following a map on a sunny day is much more relaxing since it is easier and everything is clearer.

Throughout my life as a pastor's kid and as a pastor, I have journeyed through many griefs of my own and alongside so many people on their journeys. I've studied the Bible, I've prayed both angry and confused prayers, I've wrestled with the questions, and I've wept with those in their questions. I have felt helpless. I have read books. I have asked more questions. I have seen people draw closer to God in the midst of tragedy, and I have witnessed some reject God wherein tragedy was the catalyst for abandoning their faith.

Often the field of psychology gets a bad reputation in faith circles, but throughout my studies and life experience, I see over and over the findings of psychology and neuroscience confirm biblical theological principles, not contradict them. This book explores both the biblical and psychological principles of our humanity that give light to how we were created, and therefore, how to pursue healing and restoration when we have had to survive the storms of grief. The sections of the book often bleed into each other, much like the grief process isn't neatly progressive or linear.

How you view God affects how you navigate the storms of grief in your life. Experiencing bereavement is a type of difficulty that can break us. And each story of loss is unique. Throughout this book, we will be looking at processing grief through the picture of maneuvering through a storm. Sometimes we can see the storm slowly rolling in and attempt to prepare for what is coming and seek shelter. Other times, the storm hits out of nowhere, and we are especially vulnerable. Some storms are brief; others are long and terrifying. A biblical foundation gives us secure footing both when in the storm and when processing a past storm.

The word "theology" means the study of God. In the Christian context, the terms "theology" and "practical theology" can refer to your personal beliefs of God based on your studies and how you practically apply those studies and beliefs to your life. Throughout this book, we will study biblical examples of grief, healing, human experiences with emotion, and God's character to build a personal, biblically based theology. We will also discover how current advancements in psychology and neuroscience give language for what goes on in our minds and hearts during loss. Though many examples will apply to losses of many kinds, we will especially explore what this looks like after the death of a loved one.

I didn't realize that by writing this, it would cause me to confront yet deeper layers from my own grief story. I didn't realize I had more tears to cry. I didn't know there were more pieces of pain for me to sit with. But reading this book and wrestling with these principles will bring it all to the surface. If you are in immediate bereavement, you may not be ready to engage with this book. It is okay to put it back on the shelf for a bit and come back to it at another time.

Admittedly, we are writing two different things, but I can so relate to Paul with this thought, "For I wrote to you out of much affliction and anguish of heart and with many tears, not to cause you pain but to let you know the abundant love that I have for you."[1]

I wrote this for you not to bring up pain for pain's sake, but to help assess where the damage is. If we aren't honest with our belief systems and wounds, we won't be able to pursue healing. It is my hope that this book gives you permission to process your pain, wrestle with your questions, and ultimately, see how to overcome the overcast seasons of life.

What we believe about God matters. Always. But especially when we're grappling with the darkest pieces of life. What we believe about God determines how we weather the storm. And admittedly I'm competitive to an unhealthy degree. But in this way, my stubbornness has helped ground me in the unrelenting belief that we will see the goodness of God in our lives— no matter what it currently looks and feels like.

I'm cheering you on.

SECTION ONE

GRIEF & INTELLECT

YOU WERE NOT
DESIGNED TO
EXPERIENCE
GRIEF.

CHAPTER ONE

SENSELESS

The moment I saw my mother's stomach meet her thighs as her body crumpled in half, I knew my father was dead. I was too far away to hear what the sheriff was saying, but I knew. It didn't make sense of course, but there was no denying the reality that I now lived: my dad died.

My dad and I had breakfast together that morning, just the two of us. The day was sunny and bright—typical for a Florida summer. By late afternoon, the storm of grief appeared out of nowhere, and it was eerily dark. In that one moment of witnessing my mother's reaction and realization striking me, I was emotionally flooded as the waters of grief drowned my young heart. In less than ten minutes, I pictured the rest of my life without him and how he wouldn't be there to teach me to drive, to walk me down the aisle at my wedding, and to hold his grandchildren.

I was in an immediate mental fog and didn't know what to do. It didn't make sense. We had just seen each other hours before.

He was healthy. He was a man of God. Nothing made sense. How could he just be gone?

In the months that followed, the fog continued. I would hear his voice in a crowd, or swear I saw the side of his face in a stranger's. My mind and heart were grappling for something that made sense to anchor me in the storm. But no amount of hunting for logic yielded stability or reason.

The adjustment from life with someone or something you loved and valued to life without can be jarring. Even if the death, loss, diagnosis, or break-up was a bit more expected, most people aren't ever really ready for it to occur. We all face denial in the sense of adjusting to a different life that we did not sign up for and sometimes forget we have to make that adjustment.

Why is the concept of death so hard for us to mentally grasp? Why are some diseases incurable and some disasters unpreventable? Why is cancer or sickle cell or stroke or COVID-19 or dementia or infertility or miscarriage so senseless?

Grief and loss are things we cannot logic our way through. It often feels so senseless. Perhaps because there is no answer that would justify the loss. Certainly there's no answer that would justify the pain. Perhaps because in the wake of difficulty, our reasoning is clouded. Or perhaps because there simply isn't any logic to death at all.

Our brains are physically and psychologically extremely complex. Picture the brain as consisting of three general function types: automatic, emotional, and logical. The automatic functions oversee things we don't think about, like breathing, digesting, and quick physical reactions like moving our arm and hand when we accidentally touch something hot. The emotional function brings rich variety to life through the ability to experience sadness and joy or passion and meaning. It is also responsible for assessing threats and keeping us safe. Finally, logic functions to help us problem-solve, live within morality, and engage in love and compassion.

Any time we are in "survival mode" or facing a threat (either physically or emotionally, and either a perceived threat or an actual threat), our brains assess the situation and create a plan in nanoseconds—almost faster than can be scientifically measured. This often results in what psychologists refer to as emotional flooding. The emotion center takes over, dampening the logic function and in some cases, the automatic function as well.

When we experience bereavement—the loss of a close or important loved one—our brain enters into an emotional survival mode. This can also happen when we experience other types of losses, such as the threat of being lonely after a break-up or divorce, the threat of financial instability after a job loss or change, and the threat of navigating uncertainty after a medical diagnosis or injury. As the emotional function dominates, our logic function is muted, leading to irrational choices, mental fog and fatigue, and limiting our ability to make decisions or process with reason. Yet, the logic function is still grasping to get back online, looking for a "reason" why things went off course.

We can grasp that if someone were to stand in a field during a lightning storm, that logically they may get struck by lightning. But more often the tragedy, loss, and death we all face doesn't have such apparent correlation. There isn't an obvious logical reason.

In order to more fully develop our understanding of the human grief-processing experience, we must examine our human origin story. This will help us understand how God designed our brains to function and give us a picture of what this would have looked like for humanity. Biblically, this is an important context because we do not have personal experience as a pure creation in the sanctity of original Eden. We only know the pain and challenges of our world currently. So let us begin "In the beginning…"

In the creation account starting in Genesis 1, we read that at the end of each moment of creation, each day of design, "God saw that it was good."[1] His creation had no pollution, no jealousy or selfish motivation, no tainted cells, no accidents, no illness, and (I'd personally like to believe) no roaches. He created paradise. And on the sixth day of creation, after God made mankind in His image, He saw "that it was *very* good."[2]

I quite like that. Imagine God's internal dialogue. "Galaxies of countless stars? Good. Majestic mountains with lush flowing rivers? Good. Perfect breeze and birds with the ability to harness the breeze for flight? Good. Every color of fish imaginable? Good. Human beings, male and female, wearing flesh with thoughts, emotions, and breath-filled lungs to reflect My image, to walk alongside Me and care for everything I just created? *Very* good."

Clearly the visuals of earth were good. I have to imagine the vibrant, unpolluted smells of salty ocean air and cedar pines and delicate jasmine flowers were intoxicatingly good, too. And that the sun always kissed the perfect degree of warmth and comfort on human skin while they explored silken paths of grass meadows under their bare feet. Can you hear the breeze? And the cheerful call of a nightingale? (If you can't, you should YouTube it, but be warned: it is mesmerizing.) Just imagine how good the food tasted! It was created by the command of God Himself, so each fruit, vegetable, nut, and seed were at peak ripeness bursting with flavor, nutrition, and rich satisfaction.

Adam and Eve are the only two humans on the planet who got to experience sensory paradise on earth. I wonder how they felt. I wonder if they realized the magnitudinal privilege they had. I wonder if they even recognized it because it was just their normal. I wonder if they engaged with their day-to-day life like I did as a teenager, picturing how much better life would be when I was in charge of it. And then when I moved out on my own, I learned what bills were. Oh, to go back to the more innocent, care-free, trust-filled days.

By Genesis 3, the human experiences of secure connection with God, internal peace, endless comfort, satisfied contentment, harmony with nature, security in identity and body, integral nourishment, impeccable virility, and innocence in thought and sexuality just...*ended.*

When God gave humanity dominion over the earth, His sole boundary and instruction was to enjoy every kind of fruit, except from the tree of the knowledge of good and evil.[3] Prior to the temptation from the serpent, we have no biblical indication that either human was ever allured by sin. They lived in pure joy and contentment. The serpent introduced deception and confusion into God's very good design. Humanity now, in this sin-filled earth, contains the ripple effects of this original sin in everyday moments we may not always catch. For example, since we no longer walk with God in Eden today; we now receive communication from Him through the Bible. The Word is full of promises and privileges as well as healthy boundaries God asks of us as His children for our protection, benefit, and flourishing. The boundaries God outlines aren't always approved by mainstream culture, and over time, sinful rebellion has pushed back. Isn't it interesting that when God gives us the freedom to enjoy hundreds of things, it is now the natural human fixation to focus on the one boundary? It's like seeing a wet paint sign and needing to put a finger out just to see if the sign is accurate or not.

In Eden, as God laid out His expectations to Adam and Eve, He also clearly explained the consequence in advance if they chose not to obey: *"the day you eat of it, you will surely die."*[4] This sounds a bit extreme. No second chances. The immediate result of sin would be sure death.

When Adam and Eve (who were together, by the way) willfully chose disobedience and ate the fruit despite God's instructions, they brought a flood of consequences and curses not only onto themselves but each generation to come. Unfortunately, that means you and me. And alas, it extended onto all of creation as well.

Not only was the serpent cursed for what he did (fair!), but to address the humans' nakedness, God provided garments of skins[5] to appropriately cover the shame they felt in their exposed bodies. Adam and Eve had made makeshift coverings from fig leaves, but the sap from the fig tree can burn human skin twenty-four hours after exposure. I suspect fig sap didn't do that before the fall. Even the skin clothing seems senseless at first but perhaps there were no bad weather days before sin, and God knew what His children needed in order to be protected in the days to come. At the very least, God knew their most sensitive places shouldn't be in contact with poison from the fig leaves, and He generously provided for them despite their defiance.

God did not create death on earth as we know it. It didn't exist when He created us in His image and saw that creation was *very* good. Death is not good. And death did not occur until after sin did.

The serpent convinced Eve that, contrary to what God said, if she ate the fruit, she wouldn't die.[6] I have to imagine that when she swallowed that first taste of rebellion, sweaty palms and heart pounding in her chest, she felt deceived by God. *I didn't die,* she may have thought. So naturally, Adam followed suit because he imagined God was keeping something from him. What they didn't realize was how their actions caused death to be put in motion. For the wages of sin is death,[7] or as James 1:15 (ESV) puts it, *"Then desire when it has conceived gives birth to sin, and sin when it is fully grown brings forth death."*

Humanity didn't see death as an immediate consequence. Just like they couldn't see the other curses of the pain of childbirth, the longing for a man's approval, or the need to till the ground and plant and water and harvest with not much yield for the labor right away.[8] Yet, God was indeed speaking truth the entire time. It is with this perspective that we can start to understand His instructions are not to withhold good things from us, but rather to protect the good things He has placed within us.

When God created humankind in His image, He did not create us with death in mind. With this perspective, we can reasonably conclude that the human brain was not designed to process death because it was never meant to experience it.

This is why processing grief makes no logical sense. This is why navigating the death of a loved one hurts every fiber in our bodies. This is why it causes breathlessness, steals our energy, dulls our interests, and wounds our souls. We cannot fathom it. We weren't designed to. It is not logical, meaning we cannot logic function our way through the storm. Our brain goes numb to the flood of emotions that drown our very being because we were never meant to experience death. The initial numbing is the only way our brain knows how to protect us from this unthinkable experience.

I think we deny accepting death because it defies the very nature of God within us. We don't like it because it's not like Him. We don't like it because it was never meant to be.

You were not designed to experience grief.

For centuries, mankind has sought to study and understand how the human brain operates. It is only since the 1950s that scientific advancements have begun to allow us to more fully explore, observe, and monitor dynamics happening within the brain. Yet there is still so much unknown, so many things scientists simply estimate, and there is much yet to discover. The field of neuroscience fascinates me, and each year, new discoveries and evidence of how God magnificently designed us are on full display. So many studies and publications also confirm what the Bible has instructed us for thousands of years.

For example, did you know that what you believe about God actually has the ability to shape your brain? I am not speaking metaphorically. The literal thoughts you think inside your mind about God alter the shape of the brain inside your body, and scientists can measure these changes in shape and neural pathways. This completely blew my mind. The thoughts I think shape the physical organ of my brain. But as I sat with this concept, it actually wasn't so surprising to me.

God created the universe in Genesis 1 by speaking nearly everything into existence. Though we don't know all the intricacies of God's "psyche," I know our own words are formed first within our thoughts. Our internal dialogue has great power, and the words we speak from that place hold just as much. No wonder Proverbs 18:21 instructs that life and death are in the power of the tongue. God spoke creation, but then He formed and breathed into humanity. We are fashioned like our Creator with the power of His breath, and our thoughts and words have the power to create and destroy—even on a neural level.

Research has long existed regarding creating or losing brain cells in regard to learning foreign languages, athletic skills, and instruments. Interacting with information or a skillset repeatedly strengthens neural pathways in our brains, therefore reshaping our brains. This is what athletes and musicians commonly refer to as muscle memory. Over the last two decades, we have started to see research done on the power of meditating on the truth of God as a way to improve our mental health (or our mental muscles).

Dr. Andrew Newberg and therapist Mark Robert Waldman's research indicates that the practice of meditation is associated with positive brain changes.[9] They note the most productive changes were seen when people meditated specifically on a God of love. This type of meditation indicates growth in the prefrontal cortex, located right behind your forehead. This is part of the logic function of the brain where attention span, reasoning, and the ability to engage the gentle experiences of both giving and receiving genuine love and empathy reside.

MRI scans measured brains before and after a month of daily meditation on a God of love and the follow-ups directly correlated with measured increases in physical health, including the reduction of stress hormones.[10] These studies demonstrate that meditating on a God of love calms the amygdala and limbic systems (the emotion function part of our brain responsible for survival and responding to threats). Incredibly, clarity in thinking and memory improves as well. Psychiatrist Timothy Jennings says, "In other words, worshiping a God of love actually stimulates the brain to heal and grow."[11]

In contrast, meditation on any other god-concept, one of vengeance, wrath, punishment, or anger did not result in these wonderful medical improvements or any healthy brain growth.[12] In fact, the opposite effect occurred as the fear centers of the brain were stimulated and participants' brains went into alert mode toward the god-concept they meditated on. Some researchers conclude that meditation of this sort is damaging to the brain.

This is why our practical theology in grief is so crucially important. When we are in pain, our reasoning is clouded and we can't see things clearly. This can lead to seeing a distorted image of God amidst the storm. If our foundational beliefs about God are not biblically accurate, they will inform our grief journey in destructive ways. If we believe lies about God, Dr. Jennings explains, "unhealthy neural circuits get fired and grow stronger, the prefrontal cortex is damaged, love is impaired, and fear is inflamed."[13]

Even when we have a biblical view of God, it doesn't mean we always understand why we experience pain, and where He is amidst that pain. It also doesn't mean we feel love for Him through the pain. Admittedly, there are many times on the grief journey where we can feel isolated from God. God can feel so distant because our emotions are already frayed and disorienting. There are times where our prayers can feel unanswered or we aren't inspired to pray at all. Some of us may attempt to run to God for comfort and others may attempt to shy away from Him in our anger and disappointment.

Our losses, which changed everything physically and emotionally, also changed us spiritually. This spiritual impact must be acknowledged in order for us to actually heal. Though we may be tempted to try to logic and reason our way through grief, it must be engaged emotionally and spiritually in order for us to actually get *through* the storm.

We were never designed to experience death, sickness, or loss. However, in His loving kindness, God made a way for us to navigate through these earthly experiences with Him.

Hope is not lost. Even if you can't quite sense it.

CHAPTER TWO

RUNNING IN SAND

There is more to explore in our origin story.

"And God said, Let us make man in our image, after our likeness." (Genesis 1:26 KJV)

Because we are made in the image of God with His likeness, we carry His nature within us. We might be mindful of what we think and say if we actually believe our words and thoughts are capable of altering our minds and impacting the brains of others. Yes, sin tainted this to be sure, and we now also carry the sin nature within us. But I often see many people misappropriately categorize certain human traits, particularly emotions, as being sinful or unhealthy.

One example of this is how anger is viewed. Many people will believe they "shouldn't" feel angry. Or if they do experience anger, that they are a bad person, an immature Christian, or otherwise unhealthy. Ephesians 4:26 (NIV) addresses this succinctly, "In your anger do not sin." Personally, I am grateful for this verse as I regularly feel anger. Biblically, experiencing anger is not a sin.

What we *do* with our anger can be sinful or harmful, though, and we are responsible for our behaviors and words when experiencing anger.

Another example is jealousy. Our typical human experience with jealousy is likely to lead to sin by stirring up envy and coveting. However, we also have biblical examples of how anger can be righteous and jealousy can be godly.[1] These are examples of how our emotions are very complex in nature.

Even sadness can sometimes be associated with a lack of faith or lack of gratitude. Those thoughts could sound like, "I shouldn't be sad about this change in my life because of all the good things I *do* have." Or, "Saying I'm sad about my diagnosis sounds like I don't trust God will heal me, so I'm just going to speak in faith!" Certainly faith is necessary, but denial of sadness does not make it untrue or make it disappear.

If "negative" emotions are viewed as unhealthy or societally viewed as weak, no wonder we have such a hard time navigating grief—which spurs an array of various emotions daily. Throughout Scripture, we read about God the Father, the Son, Jesus, and even the Holy Spirit experiencing and expressing emotions—even ones we tend to categorize as "bad" like anger and jealousy.[2] This is a crucial foundation to engage our own human wrestle with emotions because God's emotions are perfect, not tainted by the confusion of sin.

Once again, we must go back to Eden and picture Adam and Eve in perfection. They were created in God's image with all the range of emotions we experience today—with the exception of just a few, like shame, insecurity, and guilt. Remember when God looked at all He had made? "It is good." And when He looked at humankind He said, "It is *very* good."

He wasn't just labeling their human, fleshly form as good but everything about them, including their emotions and internal world. Before sin entered the story, we read Adam was apparently delighted the first time he saw Eve. Adam and Eve did not feel shame, and Eve understood what pleasure was since she assessed the forbidden fruit to be appealing.[3] We also know the humans had an emotionally pure connection with God and with each other.

God's emotions are always utilized for His glory and the good of His children. I have to imagine His design then was for emotions to enhance our experience of life and the creation He gave to us, for emotions to give us indications and information, and for us to use them like He does: to glorify Him and honor others.

It is hard for us to picture an internal world that is perfectly pure and holy. Often our emotions incite war within ourselves, and sometimes with others. We first witness this war at the first temptation to sin. The serpent asked, *"Did God really say you must not eat the fruit from any of the trees in the garden?"* (Genesis 3:1b, NLT, emphasis added). Clearly this question and the way it was worded unlocked a flood of internal turmoil in both humans. The serpent quite literally engaged in gaslighting Adam and Eve, causing them to question their memory, their judgment, and offering the path of independence leading to perceived power rather than trusting that God had their best interest at heart. Sin always causes confusion.

In an instant, this first disobedience introduced sin into God's very good creation. Sin didn't just wash over the exterior of creation but penetrated to the interior of our souls, thoughts, and feelings. Because of sin, our emotions are now intertwined with confusion. God's beautiful creation of emotions became susceptible for flooding, overactivity, and dysregulation of the human mind. This is where emotions and logic fell out of harmony and into conflict. What was originally designed to be a celebration of life put us into high alert and survival mode due to sin. This death of innocence and joy in thought is one that grieves me deeply. Our emotions now can drive us inevitably down the path of independence and self-sufficiency, which brings harm to ourselves, others, and ultimately brings us to dishonor God.

We were born into sin. It is not our fault that our emotions are not naturally in healthy alignment. However, like any other disease we were born with, we must seek the cure or else we will certainly deteriorate.

So it is only natural, then, in the wake of grief and loss, to have to process our emotions— especially the ones we may tend to categorize as "bad." To wrestle with thoughts, feelings, beliefs, lack of belief, and desires to believe. We especially must wrestle when these emotions conflict with each other or when our emotions conflict with our logic and belief.

I don't know how you handle conflict, but personally, I have never been into UFC, WWE, or anything like that. (Clearly, because I don't know any more initials to describe that sport.) In my home growing up, we didn't have too many external, physical conflicts. Once my older brothers play-wrestled in the hall and one butt-sized hole in the drywall later, that never happened again.

I am more of a personal expert with internal conflict. I can be an overthinker, and I'm a recovering perfectionist. In weakness, I can play things that happened over and over again in my mind, reliving the pain, getting offended all over again, analyzing what I could have said or done differently, and trying to figure out the other person's motivations or intent.[4]

I once had a dream where my boyfriend and I fought, and upon waking, I was so hurt that I used a sour attitude with him for several hours the next day. Once he discovered I was mad at the dream-version of him, he didn't know if the real-version of him should be angry or relieved. I engaged with a false character trait of his, and it put a wall between us. The fight didn't happen, the wound didn't occur, but I was feeling and behaving as if it did. Thankfully it all eventually worked out since he ended up marrying me.

When we face difficulty, we inevitably wrestle with thoughts, emotions, and yes, even how we understand God. This wrestle shines light on where we may be engaging in falsely perceived character traits of God. And sometimes we wrestle with God Himself.

Jacob of Genesis 32 had a pretty notable wrestling match with God. He lived a rough-and-tumble life of deceit and self-preservation—but also reverence for God. They wrestled all night and finally at sunrise, Jacob declared, *"I will not let you go unless you bless me."*[5]

If Jacob sat before me as my client, I would reflect that this kind of declaration is an example of using stubbornness to work for you rather than work against you, even if it was foolishly bold. God responded, *"Your name will no longer be Jacob, but Israel, because you have struggled with God and with humans and have overcome."*[6] He got his blessing.

Wrestling requires physical proximity. You must be close to work it out. I suspect we internally wrestle because it brings clarity to our thoughts, but I also believe it is an invitation to closeness with God. We are seeking logic to our pain, yet when we lean into God during this struggle, He meets us emotionally and spiritually in the storm.

Several years after my father died, I was engaged to that sweet, understanding boyfriend I mentioned earlier, Justin. It was such a happy season, full of hope and dreaming of the future together. Until grief swept in like an avalanche.

Our close friend and a fellow pastor on team at our church, Dave, was the fiftieth person in the world to be diagnosed with one of the rarest forms of cancer: lymphoepithelioma.[7] He was in his twenties and his new bride, Sheena, was pregnant. All our hearts were broken and wrestling with faith throughout the guessing game of a treatment plan. Having been close to them, I got to see Dave's wrestle with God up close.

Throughout the multi-year journey, Dave recorded his no-filter thoughts. At one particularly dark season, he asked, "Do I love God more than I love my health?" He didn't reach his conclusion quickly or flippantly, but after an intense internal wrestle he was able to answer yes.

This was not a light answer. If for nothing else, then for his one-year-old daughter. Against doctor's recommendations, Dave checked himself out of the hospital for a couple hours just to surprise us in attending our wedding. A few months later, we were on the floor of his living room all night, clicking his morphine pump every eleven minutes because he was too weak to do so and in excruciating pain. Dave died three months and seven days after our wedding. And with this being the first person my new husband had ever lost, and witnessing my friend Sheena go through my personal nightmare of being widowed, grief killed what I pictured our joyous first year of marriage to be.

I have been walking with Jesus for a long time, and some of the defining moments in my faith have come from the most difficult times in life. It can be confusing when you pray faith-filled prayers and they seemingly don't get answered, or they don't produce the way you expected them to. It can be hard to wrap your mind around the evils of injustice while serving a God who demands justice. I really crave answers, but I have yet to find a verse in the Bible where God promises to neatly answer everything.

What we do have biblical evidence of is that God promises to walk with us so we are not alone in our suffering or storms.[8] God doesn't swoop in to clean up the mess like a magical genie, but rather, He offers His hand to steady us amidst chaos and heartache. Though His peace and stability do not neatly answer all our questions, the more we experience that peace, the more confidence we have in our relationship with Him. Some storms are more challenging than others, and it is the deeply heartbreaking moments of life that can tempt us to step away from that sturdy foundation and from walking with Him.

These are the times when it is so tempting to blame God. Consequences for my own dumb or sinful behaviors make sense. But experiencing painful ripple effects from things that are totally outside of my control? It's not fair! He *could have* stopped the hurricane. He *could have* healed my loved one. He *could have* protected that person. And theologically, this is all considered correct. He could have. However, recognizing that sin has permeated the very fiber of our solar system, we have to embrace there are ripple effects we all will feel from humanity's choice to engage in sin. I believe witnessing these ripple effects and how they impact us breaks God's heart because it was never His intention for us to experience the death and decay of sin.

The kind of faith that anchors you in God's character being one of goodness is not easy or simple amidst turbulent storms. It takes great boldness like the three Hebrew young men who were threatened to be thrown into a fiery furnace if they didn't worship a statue along with the rest of culture. They stood and declared to the ungodly king, *"If we are thrown into the blazing furnace, the God we serve is able to deliver us from it, and he will deliver us from Your Majesty's hand. But even if he does not…"*[9]

Even if He does not. That is hard to sit with.

Being the realest of real, I felt I deserved a pass of sorts because I lived my life morally and "did everything right" after my dad died. I stayed faithful to God through my darkest days. I shouldn't *have* to carry the overwhelming ache of a broken heart again. Being completely emotionally crushed once in a lifetime is enough, right?

Other words for crush are deform, bruise, or crumble. If you feel your spirit is weak, bruised, and deformed because of grief and loss, the good news is that those are the very spirits Jesus rescues. If you had heart disease, you would go to a cardiologist, a doctor who specializes in hearts. If you have spiritual heart disease it stands to reason to go to the only One who specializes in spiritual hearts!

Psalm 34:18 (NLT) says, *"The Lord is close to the brokenhearted; he rescues those whose spirits are crushed."*

Jesus was sent for you and me, the brokenhearted. When our hearts are broken, we must run to Jesus.

In Luke 4:18 (NKJV), Jesus declares, *"The Spirit of the Lord is upon me, because he has anointed me to preach the gospel to the poor; He has sent me to heal the brokenhearted, to proclaim liberty to the captives and recovery of sight to the blind, to set at liberty those who are oppressed."*

A few days before Jesus prayed His gut-wrenching prayer in the Garden of Gethsemane before He was imprisoned, beaten, and crucified, we see Him interact with two contrasting believers.

In Luke 7:36-38 (NLT),

"One of the Pharisees asked Jesus to have dinner with him, so Jesus went to his home and sat down to eat. When a certain immoral woman from that city heard he was eating there, she brought a beautiful alabaster jar filled with expensive perfume. Then she knelt behind him at his feet, weeping. Her tears fell on his feet, and she

wiped them off with her hair. Then she kept kissing his feet and putting perfume on them."

The Pharisee was named Simon, and he previously had been a leper who was healed by Jesus. It's beautiful that after his healing had completed, he made space in his schedule to still spend time with Jesus. Oh, but the brokenhearted woman. She didn't just ask Jesus when they could pencil each other in; she ran to Him! She didn't hold back the tears. She didn't clean herself up or hide any part of her situation. She ran to Him with all she had and laid it all at His feet.

Healing is good, and it is fully available to us, but it is the brokenness of our life that reminds us we desperately need Jesus.

There's only one place to run when we're broken. When we can't get it together. We need to run to the feet of Jesus. I could only imagine this unnamed woman's heart was broken. Her reputation was shattered. It is in that posture she broke open a jar of perfume. From Jesus' perspective, we see our brokenness is a sacrifice and a holy gift. The gift of inviting Him close in the gut-wrenching wrestle.

When we experience a close loss one of the most commonly experienced first reactions is denial. There is a disbelief that the death happened, that the person is actually gone. Neurologically, this is a disruption to the salience network.[10] The salience network refers to a suite of brain regions responsible for our general function.[11] This accounts for why we may operate in fear of who else we may lose, be on guard for threats, be unaware of time, be unable to organize thoughts, have a general disinterest in normal life activities, lose our appetite, experience false guilt as if the loss was our fault, and more. No wonder our emotions are in a tangled mess during grief.

If it makes you feel any better, even Jesus wasn't immune from brokenheartedness or disruptions to His salience network. He did become fully human to relate with every single one of our experiences. On Jesus' worst days, He cried in prayer to God, and His prayers were heard—though not always answered the way Jesus would have wanted. Jesus cried and pleaded with God. In His famous Gethsemane prayer, He begged God to take away His suffering and difficulty. God can handle your emotions—even the "bad" ones. In my experience, especially the bad ones.

Within fifteen minutes of understanding my dad died, I was simultaneously hyperventilating, wailing, and "singing" a worship song. I have sung all my life and would like to consider myself a decent singer. However, I am confident that wail of worship was simultaneously the worst and most beautiful sound God has ever heard from my mouth. In that moment, God clearly spoke to me that when people face tragedy, they only have two choices: to run toward Him or to try to run away from Him.

Within my lifetime, I have witnessed both types of running as people experience the storms of grief. Attempting to run away from God can look like renouncing faith, withdrawing from community or attending church, avoiding prayer, attempting to either suppress anger toward God or spewing anger toward God without inviting Him into it, and exploring other belief systems entirely. Running toward God, however, includes the same range of emotions, but they are engaged in differently.

Running toward God in the midst of a storm looks like telling Him about your anger, asking Him your questions, or sometimes yelling at or crying with Him. Running toward Him looks like clinging to His scriptural promises even when you don't see or feel them presently. Running toward Him is making the choice to trust Him even when it doesn't make sense. It is choosing to put on the praise or worship playlist when you would rather sulk in silence. It is choosing to journal out the thoughts and prayers rather than attempt to suppress them. And sometimes, running toward Him is collapsing breathless at His feet because there isn't much else you can do.

I've never been much of an athlete, but one year, two friends and I decided to run twelve 5Ks in twelve months in twelve different cities in Florida. That may sound cheesy, but it was fun, and it was good motivation to keep practicing those three-mile jogs throughout the year. When planning our June race, we found one held in the town of St. Pete Beach. We plotted our commute and were excited about the idea of a post-race brunch near the beach. Keep in mind, the internet was totally a thing at this point but was only a few years old, and not every race advertised very many details online. When we arrived (at the race start time!) we discovered this 5K wasn't just in the city of St. Pete Beach; it was actually on the *beach* of St. Pete Beach.

We were totally shocked and unprepared to run in sand. I honestly didn't know if it was better to run barefoot or in my running shoes. And as we pulled up in the car, we could see all the runners just leaving the starting line, so we didn't have any time to pivot. We just started running from the car to the check in table to the start line while putting on our race shirts and bibs. What a sight we must have been.

As a lifelong Floridian, I had never run in sand before. That is *not* what beaches are for! That 5K was so much harder than any I had ever done before, and it doesn't compare to racing on the smooth pavement next to my familiar neighborhood lakefront path. Not only was I dodging the water line and children building sand castles (because I guess it's not easy to close a mile and a half of public beach), but it felt so much worse on my body. The shifting sand was unpredictable, so all my muscles had to unexpectedly and quickly adapt with every single step. I was fearful of rolling an ankle. That "race" quickly became a run-walk for me.

Wrestling with faith during grief is like running in sand. It's very different to believe when life is predictable and smooth like pavement than on shifting sand. But God isn't asking you to beat anyone else in the race. He's not demanding a competitive pace. He's just asking you to run in the right direction. If He's near to the brokenhearted, then you don't have to run far. You just have to run in the right direction. And when it's too excruciating to run, walk. And when you cannot walk, collapse at Jesus' feet.

Unfortunately, I don't know how long you'll need to run. I don't know the weight you're carrying. But I do know there is a God who is near and who longs to get close and hold you. The late Reverend Billy Graham summarized it in this way: "We can persevere with knives in our hearts when we allow God to carry us in His arms when we are wounded and to lead us to the time and place where He will heal us."[12]

When God's child is brokenhearted, He will do anything He needs to! It may not be on our timeline, but healing is available. He knows our pain. We can go boldly to Him and receive all we need—even if we've tried running away before. It all starts with turning around and running in the right direction.

I have learned so much about God as Father since becoming a parent. Before becoming a mother, I would hear the way people would talk about their children and parallel it to how God sees us, but at that time, I only had the experience, and therefore perspective, of a child in the scenario. It wasn't until I held our son through all kinds of scenarios, attitudes, health challenges, and my own sleeplessness that I started to gain a glimpse into God's unconditional love as a parent toward us. As Christians adopted into the family of God, we have access to Him as our Father and He has compassion on us through His holiness and perfection in a way none of us have ever experienced with an imperfect earthly parent.[13]

As a mom, I hate seeing my child in pain. When my son was three years old, he developed an ear infection while taking swim lessons. It was the most pain I had ever seen him in at that point in his sweet, little life. We prayed, saw his doctor for medication, had all the essential oils and salt socks, and whatever else we could find to do. When it is your kid, you'll do anything! Finally, in an effort to model leaning into faith, I picked up his *Storybook Bible* while he lay in his toddler bed, and I read a story of Jesus healing. My boy burst out, "When is Jesus going to heal meeeee?!" Through tears all I could answer was, "I don't know when, baby, but I know He will.

CHAPTER THREE

WHY?

The question every griever wrestles with: Why?

Why me?

Why not me?

Why is this happening?

Why now?

Why didn't God...?

Why does this hurt so much?

Why do I feel nothing?

Why did they have to die?

Why this way?

Why do I feel powerless?

Why can't I concentrate anymore?

Why am I having trouble sleeping?

Why am I sleeping so much and still feeling exhausted?

Why has God abandoned me?

Why do I feel guilty?

Why are my favorite things not enjoyable anymore?

Why has everyone else moved on?

Why this disease?

Why couldn't I stop it?

This question is still one of the hardest things for me to sit with as a friend, a counselor, and as a person. Again, since there is no logic as we discussed in Chapter One, there will never be a reasonable why. I don't think we'll ever know the "why" of it all while on earth. And we may not know the answer to every "why" in eternity either. But even if we did know why—would it really make us feel better? I suspect not. It's just easy to throw our emotions at something that can't throw back.

Even this nagging question of "why?" is part of the curse of sin on humanity. Remember the freedom Adam and Eve had to eat from any tree in the garden except one? What was the name of that one? "The Tree of the *Knowledge* of Good and Evil" (emphasis mine.)[1] Once again, we confirm that in God's very good design, our brain was never meant to *know* what evil is or experience what loss feels like. We were designed to be pure and innocent.

So what was the temptation for Adam and Eve to disobey? What was the shiny lure? Knowledge. The belief that God may be holding something good back from them, and that they were being kept out of the loop, propelled them into sinful action. Adam and Eve heard the instructions from God, and He had also made known the consequences should they choose to disobey, yet the lure of self-sufficient knowledge was too intoxicating.

To be clear, desiring knowledge is not sinful at all, but rebelliously pursuing knowledge or anything else outside of God's explicit parameters is. Once temptation was in play, it is likely the humans did not see God's instruction as a desire to protect them from pain.

Seeking a "why" to our difficulty is part of the human brain continuing to reel and grasp for self-sufficient knowledge. This is yet another example of our logic function searching for reason amidst an emotional flood. We want explanation and justification for the diagnosis, the affair, the firing, the addiction, the death, the tragedy, the natural disaster, and the suffering. We are looking for a reason to make it make sense. We want to try to fully know within ourselves. Yet, we cannot possibly know why, truly.

In Isaiah 55:9 (NIV), God makes a declaration that explains some of this conflict within our internal logic-based reeling, *"As the heavens are higher than the earth, so are my ways higher than your ways and my thoughts than your thoughts."* In the context of this conversation, my first impression is that I don't like that I won't get answers to some of my "whys" simply because God thinks differently than I do, or because there are certain things I may not be invited into. This may have been the same thought process Adam and Eve had.

Sitting with this verse, I see it as actually very freeing–I don't need to have all the answers and figure everything out neatly in order for me to trust God or move forward in life. Throughout Scripture, we see God inviting us to grow in understanding, in knowing Him, and in seeing things from His perspective. This is all based on our choice to participate of course, which can be a sacrificial choice amidst pain and unanswered questions.

If we don't know why, if we cannot even get *close* to knowing, then it is really important for us to ground ourselves and our beliefs in God solidly on what we *do* know and on what we *can* know. The Bible has plenty of examples of this participation in God's invitation to know Him and walk alongside Him through the storms of life. These examples range from people who accepted the invitation well and whole-heartedly to those who struggled and did so reluctantly.

Gideon lived at a time when Midianites, enemies of Israel, had overtaken Israel's land and were oppressing God's people for years. He lived in continuous fear of his life, fear for his family and country, and I imagine fear his prayers were unheard or not valued. In Judges 6, an angel appears to Gideon, whose first question was *"if the Lord is with us, why then has all this happened to us?"*[2] Interestingly enough, the angel never answers that question directly, but instead instructs Gideon on what to do. Despite his fears and self-doubts,

Gideon obeys and God uses him to become one of the greatest leaders in Israel's history. Even though his "why?" was not answered, Gideon forged ahead in faith, accepting God's invitation to trust. Generations were impacted in healthy ways because of this choice to trust in God's character, not the temporary circumstances or feelings.

Naomi was bitter in her grief, bereaved over the loss of her husband and two sons, who all died within ten years of each other, leaving her without any source of financial income and social protection.[3] She even publicly declared that God had brought the calamity on her life. Naomi did not get her "why?" questions answered, and did not navigate grief in healthy, supportive ways. Yet, she is still named and honored in the Bible and her daughter-in-law becomes part of the ancestral lineage of Jesus Christ. I see this as a biblical encouragement that in accepting God's invitation to walk alongside Him, He can weave beauty and honor amidst our mess. I also take comfort in Naomi's example that ultimately, the choices we make in our worst days don't define us forever.

Hannah, when facing infertility, would weep year after year.[4] Her husband didn't understand the depths of her pain and asked her why she was sad. I imagine how isolated, lonely, and misunderstood Hannah must have felt, especially from her husband since he handled the infertility journey much differently than she did. As difficult as carrying our own "why?" questions can be, feeling misunderstood by our support system only encourages us to further isolate, and Hannah understood this personally. Yet, Hannah continued to bring her cares to God in prayer, and her miracle baby, Samuel, later becomes one of Israel's greatest prophets.

David frequently prayed in the Psalms, asking why God hid himself in times of trouble or why God had forsaken him or forgotten about him.[5] David had already been anointed as king for years at this point in his life despite not yet stepping into that position officially. He was regularly being chased in assassination attempts by the reigning King Saul at the time and David lived in survival mode for years before seeing Samuel's prophecy and anointing come to pass in his life. Yet he did indeed see God's promises come to pass, even though it may not have been in the way David initially pictured and certainly not the timeline he may have imagined.

Even *Jesus* and His earthly family asked "why?" multiple times. When He was twelve, His parents, Mary and Joseph, left the festival in Jerusalem to travel the several days journey back home and just assumed Jesus was with someone else. After a day, they realized He wasn't there. After three days, they found Him back at church listening to the teachers and asking them questions.

After fake-smiling at the teachers and grabbing Jesus by the shoulders (my imagination), Mary asked, *"Son, why have you treated us like this? Your father and I have been anxiously searching for you."*[6] (Like Jesus left Himself behind on the journey?)

But then Jesus responded, *"Why were you searching for me? Didn't you know I had to be in my Father's house?"*[7] Twelve-year-olds have no chill and no fear. They just say whatever they want. In this example young Jesus used the question why to provide the very logical reasoning that He was fulfilling His purpose on earth being about His Father God's business. However, in that moment, I imagine His logical response did little to soothe His earthly parents' frayed nerves and anxiety. The logic did not alleviate the emotional overwhelm.

But later in a very different way, as an adult on the cross near His dying breath Jesus cried out in anguish, *"My God, my God, why have you forsaken me?"* as a tidal wave of suffering and loneliness flooded Jesus for the first time ever in this way.[8]

Jesus was actually quoting a lament from David as these words originally appeared in Psalm 22:1. Perhaps Jesus was harkening back to a "why?" that wasn't answered hundreds of years before Him. Jesus is described as a man of sorrows acquainted with grief and fully understands our human experience.[9] Fully God in that moment, He logically knew the answer, and fully man in that moment, He felt the dissonance of not being able to rationalize the pain.

Why?

Sometimes we ask "why" and we don't even expect a real answer. Ask any child why they threw their food, or didn't put on their shoes, or colored on the furniture. The answers will usually be along the lines of "I don't know" or "Because I wanted to." Neither of those responses are satisfactory to the exasperated parent or caregiver.

Because we actually don't care about the why. We're just upset that we have to deal with the aftermath. I don't want to have to scrub crayon off a wall. I don't want to be inconvenienced or slowed down. I don't want to hurt. I don't want to grieve.

There is no logic in much of a two-year-old's behavior just as there is no logic functioning in grief, loss, and tragedy.

Other times, we ask "why" with the expectation of elaborate intention. But sometimes there still aren't satisfactory answers. It's like asking my husband, "Why did you park there?" when the subtext is actually, "I think you should have parked over here where it was closer to the entrance so I wouldn't have to sweat so much walking in the hot sun." In the overheated moment, I actually don't care why he did it because whatever the reason, it felt inconvenient to me and therefore "wrong."

When we ask our why questions directed to God, we are seeking to understand something about Him and simultaneously wanting to give our own idea how the situation could have gone better. If our brains cannot "logic" grief, if grief has no stages or systems, we are left to wrestle with motivation. Why would God be motivated to cause or permit or allow this to happen? If He really is all-powerful, He could have prevented it. If He really loved...

It can be scary to really sit with this question in grief. If we do, will our whole worldview crumple while we're already dealing with a life that has fallen apart?

It is really natural to ask the question "why?" more than once. With our logical reasoning, we can recognize that asking this question is normal. However from our emotional reasoning, it can be sacrificially difficult to process each layer of why we ask "why?" Digging into the layers exposes uncertainties and unhealed spaces along the processing journey. Yet if we don't honestly engage both our emotions and our faith, we can get stuck in a downward spiral of "why?", which makes it much more difficult on ourselves to recover.

If we don't let ourselves go deeper than the surface question of "why" to the darker, uglier questions and emotions, we can get stuck, obsessed, and bitter. We're better off acknowledging all our emotions as God created them and engaging with them— wrestling with them the way only someone in close proximity with God can; either on our own, sometimes with a counselor or pastor, and certainly with God Himself as well.

Psychologists who specialize in studying resilience note healthier outcomes for grievers who allow themselves to feel the full spectrum of human emotions. This allows us to honestly engage with the difficult emotions, but also permits us to continue engaging in positive emotions, even if only in small doses along the grief journey. In other words, we have the capacity to be more resilient through storms of difficulty when we honestly face every shade of it. This is important because engaging our emotions with God requires honesty, and many feel the need to suppress or hide difficult emotions. As my brilliant husband often says, "If you numb the bad, you're also numbing the good." We cannot separate those categories of emotion. Either we feel the whole range, or we mute most of the range.

In my story, I've asked "why?" countless times. Why did my dad die when he was a good man who loved God and did so much for other people? Why did my grandfather die when I prayed for him with complete faith for healing? Why did one young man in our church get healed of cancer but Dave didn't? Why has grief been permitted to steal so much from me?

And just when we were ready to expand our family with a baby, I simultaneously started having health issues that led to a diagnosis of near infertility. This launched a new whirlwind of questions. Why is my body failing me? If I am fearfully and wonderfully made, then why is this part of my body broken?[10] Why would God place the desire of motherhood in my heart just to have to grieve this dream?

In hindsight, I didn't actually care about the answer to the why. I was hurting in the aftermath of the difficulty.

One thing I love about the Psalmist David is how he put his emotions down on paper alongside his prayers and his worship. The psalms are essentially journals, and they are so real. I also love that he didn't just ask why God forgot about him or the circumstance, but he also directed himself. Sometimes within the same psalm, David would journal, "Why so downcast, oh my soul? Put your hope in God."[11] This is a beautiful example of acknowledging emotions as they are, but not allowing them to lead you.

There is overwhelming scientific evidence for journaling as a tool to support mental and emotional processes at any time in life, but it can be especially helpful during grief processing. Journaling is not everyone's favorite discipline, but if you are picturing it being a feminine indulgence akin to writing in a diary, I would love to invite you to shift your perspective to it being a tool of strength.

There are many different types of journaling for different purposes or desired outcomes. Bullet journaling can be helpful for brief check-ins, which makes it easier to commit to do as it only takes moments a day. Gratitude journaling helps us see clearer perspectives—that there are good and wonderful things happening in our lives, even amidst painful, difficult, or depressing times. Journaling through grief helps us track where we are on the journey and preserve good memories we want to hold onto. I created a guided Grief Journal for this very purpose to be a companion through processing grief and preserving memories.

Though we don't need to walk alone in our grief processing, we are personally responsible for pursuing individual health, even amidst life storms. One of the best outcomes of journaling is to have a safe place to be filter-free in processing thoughts and feelings, which will then provide more clear thinking for how to move forward. Just like David, this gives space to acknowledge emotions, but not allow the emotions to drive our decisions.

Like Gideon and so many others throughout the Bible, David didn't get an answer to his whys. But he gives himself instructions of what to do in order to move forward. David modeled what Scripture charges us repeatedly to do: think about what we think about, renew our mind, and set our mind on things above.[12] Our strong Creator knows that our brains are always listening, and He gave us directives in the Word to help shape our brain with His design.[13] Sin has permeated this brain-shaping capacity, too. Our brains bring variables of health, function, and reliability. As a result of sin being brought into the world, we have all now been exposed to degrees of the death of God's very good design. We have experienced or witnessed abuse and trauma. Our brains are designed to try to protect us and sometimes our traumatic life experiences can lead to overactivity or misattuned sensitivity to threats.

We know the brain is complex, but there are some things we can all understand to give language to some common experiences on the grief journey. Dopamine is a hormone produced in your brain that acts as a messenger between your brain and the rest of your body. Recent research suggests that dopamine may stabilize the parts of your brain responsible for focusing your attention on what is important in the given moment.[14] When dopamine is depleted, we may feel tired, unmotivated, unhappy, experience poor concentration and poor memory, have mood swings, decreased sex drive, and experience problems with sleep.[15]

The reduction of dopamine made in the brain following trauma, loss, and bereavement means fewer signals are being sent within our brains. Though it is easy to observe that depression and grief have many similarities, this decrease in dopamine can help explain why. Our thoughts and processing are destabilized in the wake of loss. This explains some of the feelings of brain fog during immediate bereavement.

In pastoral counseling sessions, many respond fearfully to the word "depression." Depending on our history with it, either personally or witnessing someone we love walk through it, the possibility that depression is present or has returned, can be overwhelming. Some have experienced accusations that feeling depression is a result of not going to God enough. Associating depression with faithlessness or lack of spirituality can trigger more anxiety or desires to withdraw for those who feel depressed.

There is a difference between experiencing symptoms of depression and being diagnosed with Major Depressive Disorder. Experiencing situational depression is a normal human occurrence that is shared by almost every bereaved person (therefore all of humanity.)

For a visual, look at your relaxed bicep or thigh and press your thumb into the muscle, then release the pressure. While pressing your thumb, the skin moved inward, right? You just created a temporary depression in your skin and muscle, which appropriately reacted to the pressure. After releasing your thumb, the muscle (and skin) returned to place in a typical timeline. Situational depression in bereavement, and sadness during grief, are appropriate responses to the pressure of loss that our brain was never designed to experience. Though the timeline is different for every bereaved heart, if the grief is engaged, the griever will heal. For a more in-depth understanding of the difference between situational and clinical depression, please see the Appendix.

Situational and clinical depression can exist at the same time, which makes the recovery journey longer and more complex than grief or bereavement alone. Left untreated, situational depression can progress into clinical depression. This is why it is important to acknowledge where we are and follow through with healthy directives that can come from the Bible, doctors, pastors, or counselors.

If this is particularly connecting with where you are presently at in your story, I am glad you are here. Even though I can't answer the "why?", I can suggest a few helpful practices.

First, acknowledging sadness or that you are having a difficult day is not speaking negativity over your life. Oftentimes we need an objective assessment. Reach out to a licensed mental health therapist, counselor, your doctor, or your pastor to help provide the much-needed support in the wake of fresh grief and bereavement. Referrals from your doctor, asking friends for recommendations, seeking a local grief support group, and talking to your pastor or church leaders are all ways to start that process. Not everything is a perfect fit the first time, so give yourself grace if you need to try someone new after a week or two.

Second, each day, assess what you are capable of doing to care for yourself. What does your body, soul, and spirit need *today*? Sometimes a walk or swim or however you enjoy exercising can release endorphins, which is a positive support. Nourishing our body and brain with hydration and healthy foods can help lift brain fog.[16] The starchy comfort foods can contribute to depression when they aren't balanced out.

Getting sunshine and fresh air when possible helps ground us.

Prioritizing an appropriate amount of sleep helps the brain function optimally.

And if ever you have thoughts or feelings of harming yourself, reach out to a loved one.[17] They want to care for you in every way they can! They just need to know. I have often experienced the love of God through connection with safe people.

The "why" of grief comes for us all, and it requires a lot of patience. Though we repeatedly see David write a "why?" and then immediately a self-direction statement, that doesn't mean he felt better right away or even felt different at all. Nevertheless, he engaged with truth despite the feelings and questions.

It is easy to see how we get stuck in the "why?" cycle. To combat this, when facing difficulty, we must have grounding truth to repeat to ourselves—even when we don't feel it is necessarily true. Examining our beliefs about God is essential to shape our brains most healthfully.

If you have been stuck in the "whys," may I gently and lovingly point you toward what to do instead? Remember when I said God extends an invitation to us? It is to get close to Him to learn His character. Because if we don't have a solid, biblical foundation of who God truly is, what He is like, and how He thinks and behaves, we could very easily get the wrong impression.

I invite you to step away from the why, and toward the who.

SECTION TWO

GRIEF & THEOLOGY

A BIBLICAL
THEOLOGY OF
ETERNITY GREATLY
IMPACTS HOW WE
GRIEVE THE DEATH OF
A LOVED ONE HERE
ON EARTH.

CHAPTER FOUR

LOST & FOUND

We were saying goodbye to the ocean after a great family vacation. My preschool-aged brothers flanked my six-year-old frame as we sat where water gently lapped over sand. Our small hands clutched our new tiny plastic dinosaurs we had won at the arcade that week. We each had one creature, in our respective favorite colors. All of a sudden, a big wave caught us by surprise. My young brother's blue dino got swept out to sea. We tried to scramble for a rescue, but we were all so little and the large wave retreated so quickly.

My brother was four at the time and sobbed for his dino. Thankfully, over three decades later, he doesn't have memory of this moment of loss, and it wasn't traumatically imprinted on his heart. But I remember feeling so helpless at the time that I couldn't find his blue dino, and that me offering my purple one did not help the situation. I remember how hurt he was, how nothing his siblings did could immediately console him, and how his tender grief disoriented that last hour of vacation. The little toy was lost for good.

The weight of loss can feel incredibly heavy. If grief is fresh to you right now, you may be at the stage I refer to as "scrambled brain." It can be hard to be sure of much when our sense of security and safety are rocked. When time has little meaning and obligations have faded away.

It's okay if you *feel* like running away from God. He's not mad at you or disappointed in you or looking to punish you for feeling. But it is wise to be cautious and not let your feelings become a greater force in your life than your knowledge that God is for you and not against you.

All of Romans 8 is a good read for those of us carrying grief. If this chapter was read at any time of life, a believer can get encouragement and biblical vision from it. This type of study shapes our beliefs, or our personal theology, of God. However, when read while navigating the disorientation of grief and loss, I believe there are several helpful takeaways. The first part of the chapter refers to Jesus overcoming the curses of sickness and death that were introduced through sin in Eden. The chapter also clearly admonishes us to view life through an eternal, heavenly perspective, not just simply a "fleshly" or earthly one.

The chapter then crescendos with the topic of hope, and there is a particular section I will highlight here.

"...the Spirit helps us in our weakness. For we do not know what to pray for as we ought, but the Spirit himself intercedes for us with groanings too deep for words. And he who searches hearts knows

what is the mind of the Spirit, because the Spirit intercedes for the saints according to the will of God. And we know that for those who love God all things work together for good, for those who are called according to his purpose." (Romans 8:26-28, ESV)

Remember the feeling of running on sand? Thank God we have help and don't have to do it on our own. If we don't know what to pray, that's okay, too because God Himself prays for us. This is a stabilizing comfort at a time when we can feel so lost amidst a storm of grief.

I would hear my dad quote that last verse all the time: *"And we know that God works all things together for the good of those who love God and are called according to his purposes."*

(My dad was a KJV kinda guy.)

At fourteen, wrestling with tragic grief, I threw this verse at God. In my anger (and also fragile faith), I hotly prayed, "You work all things together for good? I don't see how any good can come from this. But I don't believe You're a liar so prove this in my life."

Death itself is not good. It was never part of God's very good design. Though there are circumstances when death can provide peace and an end to someone's physical pain and suffering, death was never meant to be. The pain of grief and bereavement is not good. But can God trade the ashes of your life in exchange for beauty? Yes. Yes, He can. If you allow Him to. I cannot tell you how many times God has worked the pain of my life for good not only within me but around me and within others as well. I see it every time I get to share hope—whether that comes from preaching, a counseling session, or writing a journal or a book about grief. He keeps bringing goodness into my life from something that is so very not good.

Grieving your loss does not feel good. The loss may not be good. But clinging to God's promise and allowing Him to work *all* things together for your good establishes hope for your future. "All things" means the good, the bad, and the neutral things. It is the weaving of these things that points us to hope.

Death is not the end of life as we know it but the end of life on earth as we know it. This distinction elevates our perspective from solely embracing an earthly viewpoint. Death may not have been the "good" God created, but He didn't leave us without hope. Scripture points us to the hope of eternity and the hope of God's presence with us amidst storms of suffering.

One famous verse about grief comes from 1 Thessalonians 4:13-14 (NIV), which encourages Christians to grieve differently than people without hope, or people who don't understand Heaven. More details on that (Heaven) in the next section.

"Brothers and sisters, we do not want you to be uninformed about those who sleep in death, so that you do not grieve like the rest of mankind, who have no hope. For we believe that Jesus died and rose

again, and so we believe that God will bring with Jesus those who have fallen asleep in him."

If you're in early grief, you may have responded to this verse like the famous theologian, C.S. Lewis. After the death of his wife, he wrote in his journal, "'Do not mourn like those that have no hope.' What St. Paul says can comfort only those who love God better than the dead, and the dead better than themselves."

He also wrote "...don't come talking to me about the consolations of religion or I shall suspect that you don't understand."[1] What an honest response when your heart is in smithereens. Lewis' vulnerability in sharing the raw material of his journal is a beautiful example of how all believers can feel a measure of lost hope and faith at some point in the grief journey.

It is important to note that the Bible does not state the command: Christians, do not mourn. However, Paul admonishes that our mourning should have different tones to it compared to someone without the hope of Heaven. As a pastor who has served bereaved families and as a counselor who has walked alongside those navigating grief, I have been a witness to some of people's most intimate moments. Sometimes I am still surprised by people's various responses, even though there is no one way we "should" react to loss. People aren't formulas to figure out, and there isn't a grief checklist to accomplish.

Just as there are so many responses to grief itself, there are so many interpretations and uses of the word "hope." Even among the Christian community, the word has so many different meanings and realities. I suspect it is because we don't often use the word as it was originally created.

I hope he gets the job.

I hope you have a good date.

I hope the trip is enjoyable.

I hope I get into this college.

I hope my kids get my eyes.

I hope it all works out.

I hope you can sleep okay.

All of these commonly used examples follow the dictionary definition of the word "hope." However, each phrase could exchange the word hope for the word "wish" and the sentence would mean the same thing. However, hope is not wishful thinking. Hope is not associated with luck or strong, vibey thoughts. Hope is sometimes an action, but it's also a presence. Hope is so much deeper.

If faith is present tense and describes our confident belief in God and in His character and goodness based on our relationship with Him, hope is looking ahead *through* the lens of faith to future tense, of what will be.

Romans 8:24-25 (NKJV) describes how hope is future-oriented.

"For we were saved in this hope, but hope that is seen is not hope; for why does one still hope for what he sees? But if we hope for what we do not see, we eagerly wait for it with perseverance."

In other words, John Piper says, "biblical hope is biblical faith in future tense."[2]

Another scripture that pairs faith and hope is found in Hebrews 11:1 (KJV), *"faith is the substance of things hoped for, the evidence of things not seen."*

This scripture is a declaration of what faith does. In many translations of the Bible, the word "evidence" is translated as "conviction." We can be convicted of truths even if we have not particularly seen them. I cannot see gravity or magnetic force, but I can see evidence of their existence, so I believe in them.

Similarly, I see evidence of God throughout creation and relationships. I see scriptural promises come to pass. I feel the presence of God and His love. Since I see evidence, I am convinced and convicted in my beliefs even though I have never seen God. This is faith: substance, despite the evidence unseen.

Have you ever tried to outlast someone in a cold plunge or by seeing who could keep their hand in icy water longest? I consider myself pretty competitive, but if it was a cold plunge contest, I would lose before it even started. I have a high pain tolerance but also see no need to engage in pain unnecessarily.

Keeping one's hand or forearm in icy water leads to increasing pain of mild to moderate severity, and this is known as a cold pressor task, which is a commonly used experiment regarding pain tolerance. Though it is very scripted, a fun way to see this experiment featured is on the show *100 Humans*.[3]

In a cold pressor task experiment by Berg, Snyder, and Hamilton, they found that using hope-based interventions increased pain tolerance.[4] Hope-based interventions help participants see a path forward through difficulty. Some examples are goal-setting, creating a plan to implement the goal, and positive self-talk. The implication is that hope allows us to have greater pain tolerance without necessarily changing the experience or severity of the pain. Perhaps *this* is the importance under Paul's admonishment to grieve with hope. That infusing hope into our grief processing does not reduce the pain, but it helps us navigate the journey with more strength. Once again, modern psychology confirms what the Bible always has.

One of the most prolific voices on researching hope is the founder of Logotherapy, Dr. Viktor Frankl. In his book, *Man's Search for Meaning*, Dr. Frankl shares his observations as a Jewish psychiatrist who survived the Holocaust. He observed that concentration camp prisoners who maintained hope were the ones who survived. His particular prison camp was often the last stop for most slaves prior to death—and they all knew it. Dr. Frankl, as many others he observed, maintained hope by finding purpose and meaning in day-to-day life. The vision to publish his observations and share his budding theory gave him the drive to survive an unthinkable circumstance.

For Christians, our foundational hope is that we can actually know God, not just know about Him. Seeing evidence of God is one thing, but experiencing a relationship with Him is another. But even when we have a relationship with Him, the gloom of grief can cloud our vision and disorient how we interact with this hope of knowing Him.

One complicated component to grieving as believers with hope are some theological questions. One is the connection of a lost loved one and eternity. I often hear people wrestle out the question, "What if my loved one didn't believe in God?"

Hearing those words from an earnest heart causes me to feel a holy ache in my chest. One comfort I have clung to in this circumstance is God's promise that He looks on the heart when I can only see the outward appearance and circumstances.[5] We don't know if our loved one called on Jesus even in their dying breath. Though this possibility doesn't always ease our pain or answer our questions, it is a way to infuse biblical hope into our quandaries. There is an unknown we cannot possibly know.

Another theological concern is if a loved one died by suicide. This can make grief even more complicated, especially in regard to hoping in God. Some look at the disciple Judas' damnation as evidence for suicide resulting in a loss of salvation and thus separating a person from God.[6] However, Dr. Timothy Jennings asserts, "Judas is *not* an example of what happens to those who commit suicide - he is an example of what happens to those who reject Jesus."[7]

As one who often treats suicidal patients, Dr. Jennings further explains that "suicide is almost always a *symptom* of an illness, a problem, or overwhelming distress and not an act of sin, not a willful rebellion against God or His creation. Instead, suicide almost always happens when a person is in some type of horrible pain in which they lose all hope of escape. In that mindset, suicide becomes their only perceived avenue of escape from the pain. We help those who are struggling with thoughts of suicide by offering hope—the hope of escape from their pain. We help identify the source of the pain and provide real interventions that restore them to wellness."

In these two theological concerns, our hope emerges despite a lack of definitive knowledge. This is the exact opposite thing our brain so often strives for. However, we cannot know what happens in our loved one's deepest thoughts in their darkest moments. As believers grieving loved ones, hope gives us rest amidst the unknowns in their story. We can hope because those conclusions are not ours to know.

Repeatedly we see this theme of hope giving us strength to endure pain physically, emotionally, mentally, and spiritually. Hope is not good wishes. Hope is not optional but essential to surviving the overcast seasons of life.

What is your hope?

Unfortunately, we often place our hope in fragile, fallible places. Like a tiny blue dinosaur being thrashed in salt water and sand, our hope can feel swallowed up in a storm. We put our hope in our own abilities, in the treatment plan, in the medication, in our bank account or stock market, in our connections, in our hard work, in romance, and in anything else that feels like we can have control and power. No wonder we can so easily lose hope when life goes off course.

Depending on where we place it, it is easy to lose hope. But we *can* find it again.

"May the God of hope fill you with all joy and peace in believing, so that by the power of the Holy Spirit you may abound in hope." (Romans 15:13 ESV)

CHAPTER FIVE

BE STILL & KNOW

"What do you *know*?"

My husband's unblinking eyes locked with mine from across the smooth, wooden table.

"Amanda, what do you *know*?" he repeated.

We were in the middle of a collaborative card game where you must rely on each other for information with limited hints, and you cannot look at your own cards. You have to remember what your teammates tell you about your cards in order to play them in the right location at the right time. Play your card in the wrong location, and the team instantly loses. McNeils don't like losing.

I glanced at the fan of cards in my hand, all with their matching patterned backs facing me. I remembered in a previous round when my husband had told me one of the cards was a two.

"I know this is a two."

I touched the card second from the left in my hand. Scanning the table I see the only logical spot a two card is needed and play it. Though I know my husband's tone very well, it's still a relief each time I play a card correctly. Technically, I didn't *know* the card was a two. I had never seen it. But I trusted the evidence from my teammates. I had to.

What do you *know* right now? Like really know? This is a great opportunity to practice some grounding techniques. Look around and identify some things you can see, hear, touch, and smell. Grounding helps us slow down and be present.

Think of what you know for sure about God. Not what you've heard. Not what other people have said. What do *you* know about God? I recognize there are as many answers to this as there are people on the planet. That's the beauty of God!

In each of the eleven verses in the short chapter of Psalm 46, we read of the author's faith and hope in God, in God's greatness and power and presence with us, and therefore our reassurance to have healthy confidence in God. If we *actually* believe that God exists, and we *actually* believe He is with us, and we *actually* believe that He cares for us, then naturally we would have some confidence that we can move forward no matter what we face. But pain and difficulty reveal what we actually believe. Storms also disorient us and through the fog and clouds we sometimes don't know what to believe. *Saying* what we believe and *feeling* what we believe can often be two different things. Part of the grief journey is walking through the tension of that middle ground and rediscovering the biblical foundation of what we can know.

This is why I think the Psalmist wrote, "Be still, and know that I am God."[1]

"Could you please sit still? I can't tie your shoes—wipe your face—do your hair—fix your clothes while you're moving around." This plea was a common one in the earlier years of motherhood. I probably could have predicted this would be routine in the two- to three-year-old stage. But I didn't picture it continuing to be ever present in the six- to seven-year old stage.

As a type-A personality, it's hard even for *me* to sit still. And by "sit still," I mean "relax." Really hard. I am almost always "on the go" if not physically, then mentally. In fact, I have had to *learn* to rest because naturally, I wouldn't rest or play or enjoy life until my to-do list was all neatly checked off. The problem is, as soon as I check off five things from the list, I have already mentally added eight more things to the list. It can be a vicious cycle of independence, self-sufficiency, performance, and perfectionism. Though this restlessness is partially inborn in my temperament, it is also partially the trauma response in my grief story manifesting as hypervigilance.

On the other end of the spectrum, being frozen is also a trauma response. Many grief experiences are traumatic. Depending on the depth of trauma, we can experience feeling frozen and numb with shock. (Because remember, our brains weren't designed by God with the capacity to understand grief.)

And for many people, the pain of grief leads to isolation and depression to varying degrees.

A depressive kind of sluggishness is so draining, and it can feel like motionlessness in our emotions, momentum, relationships, goals, and dreams. Sometimes it may look like sinking into substances, food, fantasies, or electronics because we cannot turn off our thoughts otherwise. Our brain is attempting to shield us from feeling the entire weight of the genuine emotions that would be released if we stopped our numbing medication(s) of choice.

Restlessness is a third way we sometimes cope with grief. Trying new hobbies, shopping more frequently, moving locations, quitting jobs or relationships—all seeking relief in the movement or the lure of something new. Sometimes these behaviors are engaged in to try to move past the pain and other times because there is an overwhelm of not knowing what to do next (so let's just try all the things!).

But God asks us to be still. Not busy for busy's sake, not numb and disconnected, not restless. Being still is a skill to develop.

In both our numbness and hyperactivity, our thinking brain is shut down. First, we have to be still, and *then* we can know who God is. An emotionally regulated place is where we find peace and understanding in His character. How He thinks and moves. Why His ways are different from our ways.

And if we don't actually know the character of God, we're bound to get some very poor impressions of Him.

In the New Testament, sisters Mary and Martha and their brother Lazarus were close to Jesus. In fact, Jesus' disciple John, who wrote the passage we're about to discuss, noted that Jesus loved them. This family was dear to Jesus, and we read in Luke 10:39 that Mary sat at Jesus' feet and listened to His teachings. To Western ears, this sounds like a simple statement. A fact and location. But why would it matter where Mary sat to listen? It doesn't if it were strictly discussing location, especially since Luke didn't list where John or Lazarus sat. In Hebrew culture, to "sit at the feet" of a rabbi meant that one was a disciple of the rabbi. In verse 42, Jesus even defends Mary's right to become His disciple despite her gender as a woman and the cultural norms of that day.[2] Mary was a disciple of Jesus! Talk about close.

In John 11, the sisters sent word to Jesus that His dear friend, their brother, Lazarus, was sick. Jesus and the disciples were about a two-day journey from where the siblings lived. They got the message and even though He loved them, Jesus decided to stay where He was for two more days and even told the disciples who were with Him that Lazarus' sickness would not end in death. We don't have any details about what happened those two days, but He finally told His disciples, "Let's head over to Lazarus' neighborhood." By the time Jesus and the crew arrived, Lazarus had been dead for four days.

Jesus had conversations with both Martha and Mary where each of their immediate responses were, "If you had been here, my brother would not have died!"[3] They said what we've all probably said to Jesus when we were disappointed: "Jesus, if only You had been here, my crisis wouldn't have happened." Mary starts sobbing so all the Jews start crying. At that moment (verse 33), Jesus was deeply moved and troubled. Some versions say Jesus got angry.

At first, I thought that meant Jesus was sad that Mary was sad. But as we look at this story in context, we can speculate a few things. Perhaps Jesus was angry that the sin nature of the world caused His people to be in pain. Perhaps He was angry that those He loved even had to experience grief. Perhaps Jesus was angry because He is not limited by time as we know time, and He is not careless as the sisters made Him out to be. Perhaps He was angered by the spirit of unbelief. In His humanity, maybe in His frustration, and probably in His care for His people who were so deeply hurt, it is in that moment Jesus wept.

The Jews who followed the family from the home to the tomb in mourning were divided on Jesus' reaction. Some noted how Jesus loved Lazarus. Others expressed, "Could not he who opened the eyes of the blind man also have kept this man from dying?"[4]

Personally, I'm so glad John included notes about these side characters simply referred to as "the Jews." It displays how wide of a response we all can have to our belief in God when we are experiencing bereavement or loss of any kind. It also is a reminder that who we surround ourselves with is very important, especially when we are vulnerably recovering from loss. Our words matter so deeply both for our own sake and the sake of others around us.

If you're familiar with this story, the next few verses are where Jesus performs a pretty famous miracle of raising Lazarus from the dead. But Lazarus had been sick for several days, then dead for four days. What did Mary and Martha go through that whole time? Before they saw a response from God came a period of waiting.

Sitting in a waiting room is an almost universal, tormenting experience. Some of the most common waiting room experiences are for the doctor and the DMV—neither of which have particularly positive feelings associated with them.

Waiting is hard. Often it can feel like we're wasting time. Sometimes we're literally in pain while we wait. One of the scariest moments in our marriage happened when we were newlyweds. My husband woke up in the middle of the night in indescribable pain. I drove him to the ER with the emergency lights flashing on our Saturn Vue as I sped through our small town. We arrived and I shakily signed him in as the second of two patients in the waiting room. My husband, a grown man, proceeds to lie on the floor and scream to the receptionist, *"Please take me next!"* Granted he had a kidney stone for the first time, and without any previous experience, he genuinely thought he may be dying. When you're in a crisis, waiting is not on your list of priorities.

Mary and Martha were in a crisis. They told Jesus, "Our brother is sick!" They sent up an SOS, a flare, the bat signal, and they were saying, "Jesus, we need You!"

This passage of Scripture reveals the character and nature of God in several ways.

First, we read that Jesus received their message. He was attentive. He heard the cry for help right away. The moment we cry out to Him in pain, asking for help, asking for intervention or a miracle, He hears[5]. God values what we communicate and asserts that value in giving His attunement to us.

I'm the first one to admit it doesn't always feel like it. This is why we must wrestle with our faith. Because beliefs and feelings don't always neatly align. This is normal, especially when maneuvering the weights of pain, disappointment, and heart-wrenching loss.

Second in this passage, we read that Jesus came. But not when Mary and Martha wanted Him to. Reflecting as honestly as I can, God's timing has hardly ever matched my desires and requests. What we do in the waiting matters. If you notice anger, self-sufficiency, or jealousy arise amidst the wait, pay attention to this. It is revealing a lack of belief in God's goodness, timing, justice, provision, or presence in your overcast hour.

If you are waiting to see God's presence in your life and you don't see anything, you might be looking in the wrong place. When you don't see God moving in your eyeline, look for Him moving somewhere else. Sometimes His priorities are not our priorities, but He is still moving and working. Still, it can hurt. We don't like not getting our way. We like being the center of the universe. I imagine that Mary and Martha thought Jesus would have come sooner. Especially considering our next observation.

Third, we read that Jesus was *close*. John tells us that Jesus was about thirty miles away, or two days walking five hours each. Jesus was close throughout the whole crisis. He could have showed up sooner. He was two days away, but when He got the news that Lazarus was sick, He decided to stay where He was for two days. Jesus was close, but I'm sure Mary and Martha felt like they were being ignored. I'm sure they questioned if Jesus even cared about the message they sent, about the prayers they prayed, or about the pain their family was in.

Jesus stayed where He was, and He had to have a reason. He even explained to His disciples that for their own sake, He was glad that He wasn't there when Lazarus died. I can only imagine the disciples digesting this. "Jesus, for *my* sake, You're glad You weren't there when Lazarus died?" That seems to make no sense at all! But of course the disciples couldn't tell what was going to happen in the story.

Jesus took His time along the way for a reason. Though we could speculate many possible reasons, we may not fully understand why He chose to move slowly. Surely there were people in His path that needed hope, too. There were people along the journey who were in crisis, too. God is close to you right now—whether you're in a crisis or not. But I imagine Mary and Martha felt alone in the waiting.

Fourth, we read that Jesus cared. Lazarus had been dead for four days, and Jews had come to mourn with Mary and Martha because the sisters were in Shivah, which in Judaism is the first seven days of mourning after the burial of a close relative.[6] During Shivah, it would have been customary for Mary and Martha to not leave the house and for close friends to go to their house to share memories about Lazarus and to pray together. When Martha heard Jesus was on His way, she did something unusual by leaving the house. She stepped outside her grief to run to Jesus. Martha didn't see God moving in the walls of her home, so she looked until she found Him.

We can so often stay numb within our walls, isolated, hurt, and upset that we don't see God show up in our lives the way we want Him to. When we don't see Him at work with our small view of life, we have to get up, be vulnerable to move outside our walls, elevate our perspective, and find Jesus. I actually think the whole point of being still is to know God so we can then take action when necessary to run and find Him in the future. We must know God so we can rest more securely amidst the overcast times of life.

When my son was in kindergarten, Bakugan toys surged in popularity. I had never heard of this type of toy, and before you

Google it, I'll just help you out. They are dragon-like creatures that roll up into perfect spheres and open via sheer force or magnetic connection, making them perfect for battling and point competitions similar to marble games.

My son begged for me to take him to the store to get a Bakugan so he could play with his best friend. (Not that he needs to find an excuse to ask for a toy!) He was fascinated with the different shapes of the toys, the different point systems, and battling them out. He memorized each of his dragon's names and power capacities diligently. And then he expected me to engage enthusiastically in battle with him.

Full disclosure: I did *not* care about Bakugans, but I care deeply about my son. Memorizing creature names and point systems means nothing to me, but it means so much to him. So, against my natural proclivity, I embraced Nillious Ultra, Dragonoid, Viperagon, and many others and met my son in joyous play.

Parenthood continually gives me revelations of God's character. I truly think of myself as a child of God. This allows me to easily picture caring about something and my heavenly Father choosing to care about it, too. Perhaps God values what we value as a way to relate with us and love us.

Whether you are grieving something that others may call small, or grieving something that feels profoundly significant, God cares about it because it impacts you.

As we consider God's character, it is important to solidify the belief system that He does not cause tragedy or death. Sin wrote tragedy and death into our stories. Even some isolated cases (like Job and Jesus), where we read about God's permission in the story, still weren't caused by Him. He allows the ripple effects of sin to play out even to this day, but as we can know from our beginnings in Genesis, He did not desire for them to happen, and He certainly did not desire for us to experience them.

One of my clients, Sarah, was talking through her grief journey with me as she was processing all she went through to now carry the title of cancer survivor. She was searching for God's purpose and motivation in all the pain with the thought, "God gave me cancer for a reason." In our session, she was asking raw, honest questions like, "Did I need to have that many close calls to death?" "Did I need to go to the ICU and not know if I was ever going to wake up?" "Did the pain need to be that excessive?"

We discussed Jesus anxiously praying in the Garden of Gethsemane asking some very similar questions and sharing comparable sentiments: *"My Father, if it is possible, may this cup be taken from me. Yet not as I will, but as you will"* (Matthew 26:39 NIV). Even Jesus Himself was asking for a Plan B and to avoid the pain and trauma that was ahead in the story. Jesus was perfect and without sin; He was God in human-form, and even He did not want to choose suffering. What beautiful permission for us to be fully human in our attempt to escape pain.

Jesus regularly referred to God as Father and taught that the Father is good.[7] If we *actually* believe God is a good Father, then I have to picture the Father's posture toward Jesus in that moment. I have to imagine the Father's heart aching seeing the ripple effect of sin and how it was affecting all creation, including His Son.

Then I imagined God's posture toward Sarah in her cancer journey and in her questions. I can only imagine a good Father's heart breaking seeing His child in pain. I shared my observation with Sarah, that God has been grieving along her journey, too, and that He hates cancer, too. Her breath caught in her throat at the perspective-altering revelation: God was in pain *with* her. He wasn't observing from a distance. He wasn't waiting for her to grow in revelation as to why she was in that position. He was suffering, too, with her and on her behalf. I couldn't help but cry tears of gratitude with her.

God is heartbroken at injustice, sickness, death, adultery, miscarriage, abuse, oppression, greed, and broken relationships. This wasn't part of Eden or His very good design. And He didn't design us to experience it. Yet in His loving disposition and creative power, He can transform suffering in our lives if we permit the work. We cannot out-busy or out-numb the pain. If we lift our eyes, we see God is sitting in discomfort with us. He longs to be present in our pain. And ultimately, He is as eager for redemption as we are.

I firmly believe Father God longs to resurrect something in your heart. If you've been head-down focused so narrowly that you don't see Him moving, maybe it's time to lift your eyes. And when you see Him, could you take a moment to be still?

SECTION THREE

GRIEF & HEAVEN

Just as human brains are incredibly complex, so too, are the topics of Heaven and eternity. Many things about both the brain and eternity remain a mystery. This section of the book serves as a reference point to what we can learn biblically about Heaven and eternity. It is not intended to be an exhaustive study. In an effort to make such complexity easier to engage, I include some of my own artistic imagination and poetic language.

When it comes to matters of Christian doctrine, there are both non-negotiable and negotiable issues. Non-negotiable issues are those that are foundational to what it means to be a Christian. One example of a non-negotiable issue is the belief that Jesus is the Son of God. Departing from this fundamental belief *is* departing from Christianity.

Conversely, negotiable issues are varieties of biblical interpretation, belief, and practice amongst Christians. Negotiable issues must be handled with care between believers. We hold them loosely because we will have a different viewpoint on these issues from other earnest Christ followers. Some examples of these topics are the timeline of the creation of earth and end-times theology. Another negotiable issue is the interpretation of eternity and the details of a believer's life after we know it on earth.

The Bible teaches there are multiple facets and stages to eternity. Heaven exists right now. The Bible allows us to know some of what Heaven will be like after Jesus returns for believers,[1] but also during Jesus' thousand-year reign,[2] and even later, what God's eternal Kingdom will look like in the New Earth. For the sake of brevity, I examine a wide overview of what Scripture teaches us about eternity. I have combined many scriptures arranged topically, but in this book, I do not specifically delineate which scriptures describe which timeline of eternity. In this book, when I refer to Heaven, I am also referring to eternity, and at times, the new earth, and even sometimes to Jesus our Redeemer, all of which are heavenly.

If you desire more knowledge about this topic, I have provided recommendations for more detailed resources in the Notes at the end of this book.[3]

CHAPTER SIX

HEAVEN IS A PLACE

I grew up in church my whole life as a pastor's kid and missionary's kid. My dad was always on mission with the gift of evangelism, and he regularly spoke of eternity, so the idea of Heaven wasn't a foreign concept to my young heart. My parents founded a missions organization in my young childhood, so I regularly had the privilege to meet new people from all over the world. As my mom led a mission trip the year after my father died, I met Courtney, whose brother had died just a few months earlier.

Courtney was a few years older than me, but we bonded over our shared close losses. By the end of the short mission trip, she handed me a book with a gently worn cream cover and a note handwritten in shimmering jean-hued gel ink on the first page. That book, *In Light of Eternity*, changed everything for me. The author, Randy Alcorn, has written dozens of books on Heaven and eternity with a mix of both nonfiction, biblically based books and gripping novels with imaginative interpretations of biblical accounts of Heaven.

With so many varying and often inaccurate cultural portrayals of Heaven (think floating on clouds, chubby babies with harps, or something more outlandish like the comedy sitcom, *The Good Place*), we may have to do some deconstruction of our societal view of Heaven so we can properly build an accurate theological view. If Heaven sounds boring, why would we want to go there? If Heaven were an endless monotonous loop of predictability for all eternity, who would sign up for that? If we do not understand the beauty of God's plan for restoration, why would we anticipate it? A biblical theology of eternity greatly impacts how we grieve the death of a loved one here on earth.

Once again, we begin our discussion in Genesis since Heaven was woven into the very first verse of the Bible. *"In the beginning God created the heavens and the earth"* (Genesis 1:1, NIV). Biblically, we see "heavens" and "Heaven" referred to both as sky and as God's holy realm inhabited by angels, and where Jesus said He was going to prepare a place for us.[1] Jesus describes His Father's house as having many rooms, or in other words, a physical location with similarities to what we know on this earth.

Heaven is also the location where God's saints who have died on earth now reside and live with Him.[2] As Randy Alcorn says, "Heaven will be *our* home, because it is *God's* home, and we are God's family."[3]

What do you picture when you think of your home? I think of comfy clothes, weekly family movie nights with "Mama's

Special Popcorn" as my son calls it, friends on our couch, church family around our dining room table, game nights, good meals, and always lovely fragrant candles. I happen to be sitting at my dining room table as I write this with lo-fi music softly playing in the background. At home, I can rest. I am safe enough to feel my whole range of emotions. I dream and create and work hard. I connect with the most important people in my world here.

Interestingly enough, I just described Heaven, too. Eternity with God will be full of comfort, and we will wear clothes, have feasts, be surrounded by our heroes of the faith and brothers and sisters in Christ, enjoy music, play and laugh, lead, have responsibilities, be productive, and we will rest. Imagine never needing to question anyone's motives or be on guard because everyone you encounter is fully redeemed.

I am also looking forward to being safe enough to feel the whole range of emotions in the direct presence of my Comforter without any measure of fear or shame or the temptation to self-sufficiently suppress or temporarily soothe. John's vision in Revelation describes this experience: *"He will wipe every tear from their eyes. There will be no more death or mourning or crying or pain, for the old order of things has passed away.' He who was seated on the throne said, 'I am making everything new!'"* (Revelation 21:4-5, NIV).

How do we know Heaven is a place? First, Jesus said He was going to prepare a place for us.[4] Honestly, that's enough for me.

Yet, God is so good to provide more details and receipts for us to go through if we still struggle with the concept.

Heaven is referred to as a city, as a country, and many times by Jesus as a Kingdom.[5] These strong visuals reinforce Jesus' reference to a physical place that is quite large. Heaven has a sanctuary with musical instruments.[6] So all of you picturing Heaven with cherubs playing harps were partially right! This makes sense since we know there will be worship in Heaven, and while some of us can hold a tune without music here on earth, others of us need the holy backup of the instruments.[7] Though I am joking, I have to imagine we'll all sing perfectly on key in new tonalities and scales and rhythms than we ever could on earth. What a joyful noise that will be!

So, Heaven is a place, and it has many familiarities to life as we know it on Earth presently. The visual of a new or redeemed earth in eternity beckons measures of familiarity for us to picture and anticipate, while still containing mystery since we have never experienced earth without it groaning under the ripple effects of sin and death.

In Heaven, we will have memories from our old life on earth. In Revelation 6:9-10, we read of martyred saints crying out to ask God when He will avenge their blood. This clearly indicates they remember the injustice of their death on earth and possibly remember the pain and suffering, too. No wonder we will need our Comforter ever present to wipe every tear from our eye. And what comfort we will have in knowing we will not have any more crying or pain throughout the rest of eternity as He makes all things new in the new earth.[8]

We have all endured suffering on this earth as we know it, yet as Jesus shared in Matthew 5:4, those of us who mourn are blessed because we will be comforted by God. I fully believe we can receive this comfort now on earth, but it also stands to reason we would continue to receive this comfort in the purest form throughout eternity. Though there will be no more sin, sickness, death, or mourning in Heaven, I cannot imagine anything more comforting and restorative than being in God's tangible presence.

In Eden, we were naked and innocent until sin was embraced, and we then sought to cover our own shame. In Heaven, we will be clothed in righteousness with robes and crowns like royalty.[9] Our new clothing reflects our adoption into a royal priesthood, and it is not to cover shame any longer, for God in purity created our bodies and finds nothing repulsive about them.

Rather, our new clothing will be a display of God's goodness, kindness, and our status with eternal life as His family members. While I don't typically think of crowns (or anything else that royals wear) as particularly comfortable, I'm not worried about our heavenly crowns being burdensome (or messing up my hair).

We will all feast together in Heaven, too!

What is the best thing you have ever eaten? As a foodie, this is a tough one for me. (I also have a hard time listing favorites, but that's a different topic.) If I had to choose one thing, it may be a Tom Kha Soup in the tiniest restaurant in the streets of Miami. This was the kind of restaurant that had a line wrapped around the building on a weekday lunch hour and their strict rules included no photos and no additional orders. You had to order your entire meal from appetizer to dessert all at once, and then your service was essentially cut off! The wait on the dirty sidewalk in the Miami sunshine was totally worth it just for that soup.

For our thirteenth wedding anniversary, my husband and I celebrated with a Michelin Star meal, which we didn't know was seventeen courses long! This feast took three hours and featured every kind of protein, vegetation, texture, herb, and element. It was a full sensory experience that even included playfulness like one of our desserts requiring tweezers and a fan brush to dig up our fossil cookie through cookie crumb dust. I can't make this up!

Jesus promised we will eat and drink at His table,[10] and Isaiah 25:6 says that God Himself will prepare the feast. In the early years of our marriage, and the budding of personal websites on the internet, I created a food blog. I loved cooking, but honestly, most of my recipes were just me trying to figure out my favorite restaurant foods. I was primarily imitating and only occasionally creating or experimenting. What a contrast with this scriptural promise. I can picture the ultimate head chef with billions of stars attached to His Name, our Divine Creator, making a feast for us. I have to imagine the feasts will be creatively unique every single time—except when we petition Him to make something again like when I ask my mom to make her stuffing recipe every Thanksgiving. You know He is going to have signature dishes. And if I'm allowed to assist, I'll even make Mama's Special Popcorn for you.

In Heaven, we will be reunited with loved ones we knew and many more we've heard stories about. In addition to Jesus and some of my personal relationships, some of the first people I'm seeking out are Esther, Job, and Jim and Elisabeth Elliot.

I have loved Esther's story of faith, bravery, and determination since I was a young girl, then held a newfound appreciation for her status as an orphan in my teen years.[11] Reading through the book of Job the year after my dad died brought holy comfort. I honor his grit and unwavering commitment to keeping his hands clean and his heart pure amidst utter devastation. Jim and Elisabeth Elliot were missionaries in the 1950s and became famous when Jim was murdered by the remote South American tribe with whom he was building a relationship.

Elisabeth managed to continue building the relationship and moved in to live with the tribe two years after her husband's death. She won many of the tribe to the saving knowledge of Jesus. I have *so* many questions for her.

In Matthew 8:11, Jesus says we will attend a feast in the Kingdom of Heaven with Abraham, Isaac, and Jacob. The heroes of our faith are at the table, and they will be recognizable. First Thessalonians 4:14-17 is often referred to as the "Reunion Passage" as it describes living Christians and those who have died as reuniting simultaneously with each other and with Jesus when our Lord returns. We will know things about one another, such as knowing who was martyred for their faith.[12] We will talk and sing and celebrate in unity as the family of God.[13] One of my favorite things about my church is that it is multicultural and multigenerational. Each Sunday that we worship together feels like a glimpse of the unity and diversity we will share together for eternity.

Since July 11, 2001, I've been anticipating being reunited with my earthly father in Heaven. Two of the trips he wanted to take our family on and didn't get to are to visit the Grand Canyon and Niagara Falls. I can only imagine exploring those breathtaking sights with him in the new earth that God establishes. We know Heaven contains nature as Revelation 22:1-2 describes a river of life flowing from God's throne and flanked by Heaven's streets and the tree of life bearing fruit with healing in its leaves. (What a contrast to the fig leaf!)

While on those new adventures with my dad, I can't wait to share deep belly laughs again—the kind that make your ribs hurt. What bliss to know we will laugh with the God who created all emotions, including overwhelming joy.[14] We will also play in Heaven as indicated in Mark 10:15 when Jesus taught that in order to enter the Kingdom of Heaven, we must receive it like a child. I've never met a single child who didn't long in the depths of their heart to play.

We also read about animals inhabiting Heaven and with the curse lifted we will be in complete harmony with these creatures just as God originally designed.[15] I have to imagine that could make for some playful adventures far beyond the offerings our earth has seen lately of swimming with dolphins, pigs, or sharks, goat yoga, camel or elephant rides, or snake charming.

In addition to play, we will have opportunities to operate in leadership gifts and be productive. To some, this may not sound like fun, but let us remember we have only been alive during the curse. One of the curses Adam received in Genesis was that all Adam's work would be hard, full of toil, and sweat-inducing.[16] We have no idea what it is like to be productive without stress, obstacles, pressure, insecurity, failure, thorns, pests, lack of unity, technical difficulties, or disasters. Eternity with God holds the most pristine work environment where we can live purposefully to serve others, produce, and build—all without the decay we know of this present earth.[17]

We will build homes and plant gardens and catch fish.[18] And with so many precious jewels, there may be opportunities to create custom jewelry.[19] How cool is it that even hobbies will be maintained in Heaven? We do not need to fear boredom. We will continue to learn throughout eternity since God is infinite in His omniscience.[20]

In eternity, we are promised rest.[21] With our work not being toilsome, I wonder if we will find rest in simply being. But how beautiful to picture no more insomnia or anxiety, no looming deadlines or brain fog. I've heard it said that Americans wear busyness as a badge of honor. Some of us may have to learn what true rest is meant to be. I'm so glad God is tender and patient with those of us who are hardheaded. (And by "those of us," I mean me.)

One partial mystery of Heaven is what time will be like. We know that time exists in measures we are familiar with since the tree of life yields fruit every month.[22] We also know there is a precise timeline with Jesus' thousand-year reign before creating the new earth.[23] The martyrs are aware they haven't been vindicated yet and are asking God *when* He is going to do so which indicates they are also aware of what is happening on earth in the present,[24] and we read about silence for about half an hour in

Revelation 8:1. I heard a joke citing this verse as proof that men will arrive in Heaven thirty minutes earlier than women.

We were made for God's presence. Eden was a reflection of Heaven that you and I never got to taste. Every theologian I have come across preaches that we will feel more at home in our eternal home than we've ever felt anywhere else in our lifetime. Even C.S. Lewis, while not in the immediate wake of bereavement of his wife, said, "Your place in heaven will seem to be made for you and you alone, because you were made for it stitch by stitch as a glove is made for a hand."[25]

I can't wait to see you there!

CHAPTER SEVEN

HEAVEN IS A HEALING

"I don't think I should go on the youth ski trip," I told my parents. I was thirteen and my grandfather was in the hospital, hardly responsive after a stroke. I had saved up the money and fundraised to go on this youth trip that I had been greatly anticipating for months, but I now didn't want to leave home. What if he got worse? What if he died while I was gone?

I wrestled with my belief system at thirteen years old about God's faithfulness, healing, my faith, and my prayers.

I prayed full of faith that my Grandpa would be healed. I asked God and had no doubts at all. I *know* God is good. I *know* God can heal. I've seen it. I fully trusted God and believed, based on scriptures that simply by asking God in faith, my Grandfather's healing was guaranteed.[1] So I asked for my Grandpa's healing with no doubts at all that God would do it.

Standing at his hospital bedside, holding his soft, wrinkled hand, I asked my grandfather if he could hear me, to squeeze my hand. His freckled hand gently squeezed mine, his blue veins bobbing slightly just under the surface of his thin skin. I told him I loved him and that I was praying for his healing, and that it was done in Jesus' name.

I went on the ski trip with a much less worried mind, full of hope. That trip provided continued formative time for my faith to deepen and grow. A few weeks later, Grandpa passed away. My faith was pressed, and my heart was crushed. Immediately my mind, as ours so often do, made it about me.

"Did I not pray with enough faith? Was there a little doubt mixed in? What did I do wrong? Was there a prayer I didn't pray? Jesus said nothing would be impossible with faith. I really prayed in pure faith!" I don't remember questioning if Scripture was true, but rather, I questioned where *I* had failed.

I had lost a young cousin, a grandmother, a few pets, and a community during a move across the state at this point in my journey, but I had been so young. Losing my grandfather was the first close loss I truly felt. This is where my wrestle with God and grief really began.

"Why didn't God heal Grandpa when I asked Him to heal, and I asked full of faith?"

Oh, that pesky "why" question again. Why doesn't God heal all the time? (At least, as I understand it or picture healing.) Why do some people seemingly get healed and others don't?

It didn't happen immediately, but in the year between my grandfather's passing and my father's passing, I had a revelation about healing. Heaven *is* a healing.

In eternity, we receive our new, glorified bodies. Bodies without weakness, illness, tainted cells, degeneration, sprains, arrests, corruption, stroke, imbalanced hormones, or sluggish metabolisms (hallelujah)! Presently, we have a natural body that will die due to the consequence of sin on earth, and we will receive a spiritual body in eternity. Our natural bodies die in weakness, but they are raised in power.[2]

God made humans in His image: body, soul, and spirit. We even read of God taking human form occasionally in the Old Testament. Remember when Jacob wrestled with God so hard his hip got popped out of socket? God seemingly had to be like a human for that to look remotely like a fair fight. Additionally, Abraham, Joshua, and Nebuchadnezzar witnessed God in human form.[3] Even Genesis describes God walking through Eden in the cool of the day.[4] As far as I know, this may mean Adam and Eve interacted with God in human form. Then of course, Jesus is described as the Word of God made human.[5] He ascended to Heaven in His body as a man. Biblical examples are not just limited to God the Father and Jesus. They also include the Holy Spirit who dwells in our earthly bodies.[6]

God puts so much emphasis on our earthly bodies. Why? Because we are not just spiritual beings headed to a spiritual location, but we are fully human and fully spirit. We experience who we were fully meant to be in the holy presence of God.

From earth's vantage point we see death as a loss—and certainly to life as we know it, this is inarguably true. But we also see this sentiment of loss and pain echoed from Heaven's elevation, too, since death was never meant to be. This is why Jesus came to earth, to put a holy plan into motion to defeat death once and for all. Carrying pain in the present while also holding hope for the future is a challenging act for the grieving heart. However, Heaven has the advantage of an eternal viewpoint that sees ahead in the story, longing for the redemption that will be.

Author and pastor Jennie Lusko shares this perspective when she describes watching her five-year-old daughter, Lenya, transition from life on this earth to life in Heaven. "I realized an awful, yet beautiful tension: our worst day was actually Lenya's best day. Her death, while horrible to us, led her straight to her Savior."[7] With this lens of Heavenly honor and holy hope, let us examine two verses that are often quoted at funerals.

Psalm 116:15 (NIV): *"Precious in the sight of the Lord is the death of his faithful servants."*

1 Corinthians 15:55 (NIV): *"Where, O death, is your victory? Where, O death, is your sting?"*

In the throes of immediate, deep bereavement, these verses can almost be insulting. This is why our posture in grief is critical.

Our limited human view informs our disposition during grief. Do we attempt to balance on the quaking infrastructure of culture and emotion, or do we lift our eyes to stand firm on the foundation of a biblical worldview?

I grew up in the South and often would hear the phrase, "Bless your precious heart!" Or some variation of it. Hearing it from gray-haired church aunties and uncles, it often struck me to mean I was adorable, cute, or that I had a lovable heart. The word "precious" in Hebrew as written in Psalm 116:15 translates to "costly" and "highly valued."[8] If we were to wrestle with this verse and misinterpret that word by how it is often used in culture, it could leave us with the impression that God views the death of His children as "lovely" or "good" when this is the furthest thing from biblical truth and the evidence we have of God's character.

The declaration of death no longer having a sting from 1 Corinthians 15:55 is a promise that we will receive in eternity after Jesus makes all things right. If we attempt to proclaim this verse presently, it could very well invalidate someone's very authentic bereavement. Knowing what the Bible actually says about death, healing, eternity, and God's character allows us to walk out our faith more securely through the storms of grief.

As God's children, we must expand our view to be from Heaven's perspective. Randy Alcorn succinctly states, "The Bible explicitly tells us that we'll live forever, in resurrected bodies, on a resurrected earth.'"⁹ Present pain over death and loss is real. And the hope of eternity can also be presently real.

I didn't realize as a young teenager that God actually did answer my prayer. My grandfather is fully healed in God's presence in eternity. His healing truly was guaranteed in Jesus' name. That is not the healing I asked for, pictured, or had faith to believe for, yet Grandpa is now fully healed and whole. He hasn't experienced pain for over two decades on this earth.

This revelation gave new dimension and peace to my theological wrestle. God *is* still good. God *is* still healer. Though it brought a measure of comfort, it didn't fully take the sting of disappointment away that I didn't get the healing I wanted.

Not only was my Grandfather in Heaven to welcome his son—my dad—but the two of them have been able to meet three of my siblings that I have yet to meet. I don't know why my mom had to suffer through three miscarriages. I do know that if the first had been born, I would not have. And though my status as a rainbow baby did not erase the pain of loss from my mother, I am grateful I was gifted life on this earth, even with all its peaks and valleys. I am also grateful for the promise of Heaven that, *"Never again will there be in it an infant who lives but a few days, or an old man who does not live out his years."* (Isaiah 65:20, NIV). We will all live the full measure of our days in God's image and likeness in eternity.

One of God's names is Jehovah Rapha, which translated from Hebrew, means "I am the Lord who Heals."¹⁰ God is our Great

Physician. He is the Lord our healer. Healing isn't just something He does sometimes, it is *who* He is. He is Healer all the time. When we feel it and when we don't. When we see it and when we don't. To be in His presence in eternity is to be perfectly healed and whole.

I fully recognize this isn't always a satisfactory answer when we are in the midst of pain. But if we're able to sit with this biblical truth, it can bring great comfort and revelation. Remember when we discussed God comforting us through some earthly memories? That kind of attunement and care brings healing. He is Healer on earth, and we will continue to see Him as Healer in Heaven to our bodies, hearts, and souls.

Since I have yet to personally witness God's heavenly healing, let us anchor what we can know by reflecting on earthly healing. When we study the healing miracles Jesus released while He was on earth, we can see some patterns and some distinct lack of pattern.

One pattern we see is that invariably, He was on His way somewhere for some other purpose and someone interrupted Him with the petition for a miracle. Jesus responded so graciously and with compassion. And He always stopped to listen and make time for each person. It is almost as if He was there just for that person's request. Perhaps these just seemed like interruptions since the accounts are recorded from the disciples' human perspective of Jesus needing to get where He was headed. Your prayers and petitions are not an interruption to Him. He deeply cares for you and all that is in your heart and life.

One lack of a pattern we observe is that He didn't have formulas, checklists, or "repeat" miracles. Jesus healed some blind men by touching their eyes and another blind man He healed by putting mud on his eyes, and yet another healing of blindness with Bartimaeus simply by vocalizing the man's faith made him well.[11]

To a group of men with the (back then) incurable disease of leprosy Jesus commanded them to go to the priest, and they were healed on the way as they walked in obedience.[12] For another man with leprosy, Jesus directly touched him.[13] This must have shocked the man (and perhaps the disciples) because this was against medical wisdom of the time as the disease was believed to be contagious, but also against the religious law as touching the man would make Jesus, a rabbi, ceremonially unclean.

To some, Jesus spoke words of healing; to others He offered the physical touch of healing; and to the woman plagued with infertility and hormonal issues with constant bleeding for twelve years, her faith to touch His garment was all that was required for her healing to be received.[14]

Even after Jesus ascended to Heaven, by the power of the Holy Spirit, Peter declared healing to a man who was lame from birth. As Peter reached his hand to help the man stand up, the man's feet and ankles were instantly strengthened.[15]

The common pattern between all these stories? All these examples included someone's faith.

Though these are examples of healing on this earth, I believe it showcases God's character beyond this earth since Jesus is the same *"yesterday, today, and forever."*[16] According to Isaiah 55:8-9, God's ways are not our ways, and His thoughts are not our thoughts. His ways are higher than our ways. God has a higher, longer, eternal view of our circumstances and storms.

We know God doesn't cause trials, but He does allow them. Why? His ways are higher than our ways. God does things (or sometimes doesn't do things) according to the overall view, rather than our finite view and temporary circumstances. God is far more complex than we are. We are made in His image, meaning we are like Him. But He is not like us. It will often be challenging and sometimes fruitless when we try to comprehend God's higher ways using our limited ones. This internal challenge guides us to the need for faith, trust, and surrender.

On a family outing, my husband, son, and I entered a life-size maze. We had the whole thing to ourselves, possibly because we were foolish enough to do this at the height of the cloudless midday Texas heat. For this particular maze, you had to find four different checkpoints, then look for the exit. My husband's parents observed us from a covered watchtower above the maze while we each raced around with all our competitive adrenaline pumping. Like I said, McNeils don't like losing.

You should know our son also inherited my excellent sense of direction. He and I both separately navigated the confusing turns with ease after a few moments of running and orienting ourselves. My husband, well, he is a great driver, but never the navigator on road trips.

Not that it is the most important detail, but I finished the maze first, and our son not too long after. Okay, it actually is an important detail. My son and I joined his grandparents on the watchtower and observed my husband go in similar loops while looking for different checkpoints. Seeing the maze from the elevated view gave me the advantage to see the bigger picture and see the advantageous paths compared to my husband who was in the challenge at the moment. He eventually invited our help, and we were able to guide him to reach the other side in victory. This game was simply for fun, and we were able to laugh it off together.

In challenges with higher stakes, though, the emotions are different and often much more tender. As we discussed previously, God empathizes with our pain, feeling it alongside us and certainly doesn't laugh at us from His higher vantage point. Rather, He invites us to trust His directions through the challenge since He sees things from a superior vantage point. He invites us into greater trust in His character even while we are in the middle of struggle.

With Lazarus, Jesus does explain the "why" behind some of the variables in the story, saying the sickness and death occurred for God to be glorified.[17] The blind man Jesus healed in John 9 was also an example of bringing glory to God. In the opening of the chapter the disciples questioned Jesus if the man was blind because of his own sin or the sin of his parents. Jesus affirms the blindness had nothing to do with their sins but that the blindness was present so that the works of God (or His action and character) could be viewed through the blind man's life.

God wants to be seen through our blindness.

What a comfort this is to me that many of the trials and difficulties we face in life are not caused by God and are not the result of my sin directly, but rather the sin nature in general that has been put into motion since sin clouded Eden. Amidst the blinding storms of grief, this helps me make sense of the idea that it "rains on the just and the unjust."[18]

I have sat alongside many families in hospital rooms. Some stories lead to what we traditionally think of as healing, and other stories lead to planning funerals. I will never forget the most difficult, tragic hospital visit I have ever done. The heavy silence of fresh grief haunted the entire room, and all I could do was pray silently in my mind for an hour amidst the dark oppression. There were no words one could verbalize in that moment that would be sufficient to a family in devastation. I let myself loudly wail alone outside in the sunshine as I trudged slowly to my car.

Those most difficult moments definitely stand out. But there are also moments of light and beauty *within* those darknesses as well.

One woman in our church, Michelle, experienced prolonged grief with her mother in memory care for a decade. The entire ten years, her mother didn't even know who Michelle was. This decade contained grandkids growing up and marrying, new babies being born into the family, and a significant life transition for Michelle and her husband. This grown daughter wasn't able to share any of that with her mother. When her mother passed away, I called Michelle (who was out of state making arrangements for the service), and her words struck a deep chord in my heart.

"We've been waiting for her to be healed for ten years, and all I feel is gratitude that it's complete."

Michelle's words resonated with the truth of God's Word. Granted, she has decades of history following the Lord and her faith has been deeply rooted as she has walked through many storms. But even the most faithful can be shaken by loss. I actually believe that it is because of how Michelle has relied on God throughout previous overcast seasons that her deep conviction of hope is what rose to the surface in the wake of yet another painful storm.

Heaven is a healing. It isn't always the healing we ask for or desire, yet it is still a complete miracle with full restoration—even better than anything we could picture on earth currently since throughout eternity we get to experience the physical presence of God Himself.

Like my questions at thirteen about God not following through with the biblical promise of healing when I was faithful to do my part, so many people experience loss and view it as yet another reason to lose trust in God.

"Did God really say?"[19] This was the question the serpent asked Eve back in the garden thousands of years ago. The enemy has no new tactics and preys on the opportunity to plant doubt in our minds about the character of God.

I don't know why my grandfather, Dave, Michelle's mom, Courtney's brother, and so many others were healed in eternity and not in this lifetime. But I am confident that every prayer prayed for their healing, every tear wept in anguish, every moment of fasting, every bold declaration for restoration was heard, valued, and answered by God.

Understanding Heaven elevates our perspective. If loss was limited to our earthly experience, it would end there and of course be debilitating with no purpose other than pain. But understanding that Heaven and the new, restored earth is our *true* home gives us an eternal viewpoint. Let us not limit ourselves to the narrowness of this lifetime alone to experience healing.

CHAPTER EIGHT

HEAVEN IS A PERSON

When I kissed the face of our wide-eyed newborn son after our journey through infertility, I felt like Heaven momentarily crossed into earth. I felt similarly when standing on Israeli soil. I have felt this crossover in many worship services. Though our faith is about so much more than fleeting feelings, being able to experience the feeling of Heaven on earth is intoxicating. It is sometimes hard to describe, but it is not easy to forget.

Our church regularly hosts some dear pastor friends who lead us in an entire service dedicated to worship. If you've never heard of David and Nicole Binion, add them to your playlist right now and thank me later. They are anointed and lead worship so purely, beautifully, and uniquely. Nicole sounds like an actual angel, and David has a prophetic storytelling gift throughout worship that uniquely weaves depth and humor together.

They have witnessed multiple healings throughout their ministry, including one significant physical healing at our church over a decade ago of a young man miraculously healed from over fifty cancerous tumors in his body. Within a matter of three weeks, we saw a death sentence reversed. They are the type of people that are fun to be around and you leave refreshed from being in their presence. You can see why we enjoy hosting them as guests as often as we can.

The most recent time they visited, seemingly out of nowhere between songs, Nicole burst out singing declaratively, "Heaven is a person!"

I instantly dropped to my knees on the chilled concrete floor as uncontrollable tears formed tiny streams around me. I was so taken off-guard as I had never heard that phrase before. I had never considered it. And I was instantly deeply convicted about my view of Heaven.

In wholehearted selfishness, I had primarily looked at eternity to be the reunion with my earthly father, *above* it being eternal union in person with God. Perhaps because I have always viewed God as with me, so I haven't felt a particular sense of longing for or absence of that. Or more deeply perhaps because my view of Heaven was formed in the wake of a brokenhearted teenage girl who missed her dad terribly.

Heaven is a person, and His name is Jesus.

Consider the history of God's people prior to Jesus stepping into our neighborhood in human form. The people of Israel could not step into God's actual presence and had to give their petitions to the priest, who would go into God's presence once a year. Each family had to sacrifice animals for the shedding of innocent blood to cover their sins and a scapegoat was banished to the wilderness most often to its death.[1]

To our modern society (and animal lovers everywhere), this sounds so foreign and harsh. God is holy, and He cannot be in the presence of sin. Yet the Father sent His Son, Jesus, to step into our humanity and experience it with us in order to cover our sin once and for all. Poetically, Randy Alcorn wrote, "The God who lives in unapproachable light became approachable in the person of Jesus."[2]

Jesus came so that we might experience Heaven on earth, Heaven in Him. But His first arrival did not bring with it an elimination of heartache, sorrow, and difficulty. He beckons us to experience Heaven *in* Him even amidst the overcast seasons of life. His love and His presence is instantly accessible to us, no matter how dark and cloudy life gets.

"Who shall separate us from the love of Christ? Shall trouble or hardship or persecution or famine or nakedness or danger or sword? As it is written: 'For your sake we face death all day long; we are considered as sheep to be slaughtered.' No, in all these things we are more than conquerors through him who loved us. For I am convinced that neither death nor life, neither angels nor demons, neither the present nor the future, nor any powers, neither height nor depth, nor anything else in all creation, will be able to separate us from the love

of God that is in Christ Jesus our Lord." (Romans 8:35-39, NIV)

Nothing can separate you from God's love in Jesus. Although I imagine many life circumstances have tried to convince you otherwise.

In Jesus' time on earth, we observe something that piques my curiosity. He does not use the word "death" the way we typically do. Several times, we read Jesus refer to someone as asleep or sleeping when they were actually dead by human definition. Jesus referred to Lazarus as asleep (which really confused the disciples.)[3] We also read Jesus use that term about a young girl in Matthew 9:24. After Jesus ascended into Heaven, the disciples adopted this language because we read about Stephen "falling asleep" as he was martyred.[4]

Dr. Timothy Jennings speculates about this, too. "I asked myself, was Jesus lying? Was he trying to trick the disciples? Was he trying to create confusion, or was he attempting to open their minds to truth? I realized that Jesus was revealing heavenly light and that, if I wanted my mind to heal, I had to embrace it…In the mind of God, sleep and death are not the same. They serve very different purposes. For instance, the Bible does not teach that the wages of sin is sleep or that sin, when it is full grown, brings forth sleep (Romans 6:23; James 1:15.) In the language of God, sleep is temporary, death is permanent."[5]

In other words, the Bible uses the word "death" in connection to the enemy as we saw in Eden. Sin brings about death. Jesus and the disciples used the word "sleep" to indicate a transition for a human to go from life on this earth to life in eternity.

This is big. The sin that permeated God's holy creation in Eden brought the curse of death. Jesus came to break the curse so that we might have life.[6] Jesus broke the power of sin and death bringing life and immortality to light through the gospel.[7] Jesus Himself brought Heaven to earth so that everything as we humanly know it, is now different. Jesus did something so big, even the disciples couldn't fully grasp the depth of it in their lifetime.

The longer I walk with Jesus, the more I see His character is to provide complete salvation, healing, and restoration, yet He invites us to understand, explore, and experience more of salvation, healing, and restoration. The person of Jesus understands our humanity, our limited mindsets, our sin and shame, and He has so much patience for us in our wrestle.

On the cross and in rising from the grave three days later, Jesus fully broke the curse of sin, death, and separation from God. Instantly the disciples received such significant breakthrough, healing, and freedom from sin and death, yet they weren't aware. They didn't understand that Jesus' work was complete and that they had all the salvation and restoration they needed. So amidst the forty days Jesus was on earth after the resurrection, they asked for clarity.

Acts 1:6 (NIV): *"Then they gathered around him and asked him, "Lord, are you at this time going to restore the kingdom to Israel?"*

Clearly, the disciples thought salvation and restoration looked a certain way politically and socially.

"He said to them: 'It is not for you to know the times or dates the Father has set by his own authority. But you will receive power when the Holy Spirit comes on you; and you will be my witnesses in Jerusalem, and in all Judea and Samaria, and to the ends of the earth.' After he said this, he was taken up before their very eyes, and a cloud hid him from their sight." (Acts 1:7-9, NIV)

In verse 10 angels had to essentially tell them, "Hey guys, stop looking in the clouds. He's not coming back." I kind of don't blame the disciples. With Jesus appearing throughout the forty days, how could they know this was the last time (even though it was clearly the most epic exit.)

But the disciples listened to what Jesus commanded about staying in Jerusalem until they received the gift. They had no idea what it was or exactly how long they would have to wait. Like Mary and Martha previously, the disciples then entered days of waiting for the fulfillment of His promise and a period of grief over the loss of Jesus' physical presence.

In this waiting season, we see the community of the early church forged for the first time without Jesus' physical company. *"They all met together and were constantly united in prayer"* (Acts 1:14, NLT). We observe unity, prayerful attitude, obedience, and a posture ready to receive. This was the atmosphere God chose for the Holy Spirit to fall upon them, releasing gifts, power, and confidence to be who God has called His followers to be.

This passage speaks so powerfully of God's character, even though it may have felt God was seemingly absent in their overcast season of grief. Because of the cross, the disciples received significant freedom from sin, sickness, and death and instant and constant personal access to God for the first time since it was shattered in Eden. They received healing and breakthrough for addiction, insecurity, and anxiety.

Jesus didn't need to do a single thing more. As He said on the cross, "It is finished."[8] His work was complete. He could have stopped there because He did everything for us. Yet, here is where we see God's character on glorious display. Because of the cross and resurrection, God's work in us is complete *and* He invites us into more.

God didn't need to do anything beyond the cross, yet He promised another good gift. The disciples hadn't personally experienced the person of the Holy Spirit until Pentecost. Jesus' good work was complete, yet He invited the disciples to experience more.

We see this part of God's character all throughout Scripture. In the Old Testament, we read of a prideful general, Naaman, who lived intoxicated on his own status and power. When he experienced an essential death sentence (physically, socially, and politically) with a diagnosis of leprosy, he was urged to seek out the prophet of God for healing. God didn't just want to heal Naaman physically, but He desired to heal his pride and self-reliance, too.[9]

In the New Testament, we see Jesus didn't just heal a lame man physically but healed his heart and spirit with the declaration that his sins were forgiven.[10] The physical healings in isolation could be considered a complete work, yet God provided more than just one type of healing.

We all can testify of the goodness of God in our lives. He delivered us from something, He carried us through something, and He protected us from a lot of somethings. We all have a testimony, and your voice and your testimony matters! *And* God is inviting us all into more. Our testimony, our story, our healing, our victory is not just past; it is present. God is inviting you into more healing, more wholeness, and more victory if you'll pursue it.

This sounds so encouraging! Yay! It's complete and there's more! It kind of sounds like having the best meal of your life, then learning the chef is stocking your house with the ingredients— you're so satisfied and there's more satisfaction available.

But picture what this was like for the disciples. In those days between Jesus' ascension and the gift of the Holy Spirit, they were hanging out together praying, developing relationships, and in a spiritual cocoon, rejoicing in the freedom of Jesus.

When they accepted the invitation into that promise of more and accepted the gift of the Holy Spirit, the commission to go into all the world began. Accepting the invitation to more of God's goodness—new layers of healing in our stories and increasing authority and influence—results in more action and accountability in our lives. It is work, and it requires holy surrender.

Jesus brought Heaven to earth for you and me. He has done a complete miracle and healing work in your life already. And He invites you into more. What a divine invitation.

Isaiah 61 is an Old Testament prophecy of the characteristics the Messiah will have. Jesus happens to read this prophecy publicly in the temple in Luke 4:18 and declares that the scripture is fulfilled in Him. What does Isaiah 61 promise? That Jesus would bind the brokenhearted. That He would release prisoners from darkness. That He would comfort those who mourn and provide for those who grieve. That He exchanges beauty and joy for ashes and mourning. And that He provides garments of praise for those clothed in despair.

Practically, what does this look like in our lives? We read examples and hints of it all throughout Scripture because the disciples weren't so different from you and me. They needed a clear picture just as we do.

Recall a story we examined earlier from Luke 7, where we read of an unnamed sinful woman anointing Jesus' feet. Her tears and perfume from an alabaster jar were a display of vulnerable worship and gratitude. All this happened in the home of Simon the Pharisee who openly judged her and spoke about her to Jesus as if she wasn't sitting right there. We don't actually know what her sinful nature was, but her reputation was certainly well-known enough for the religious leaders of town to know to avoid her.

After teaching about the forgiveness of God to Simon and all those present, Jesus turns to this woman and dignifies her to speak directly to her and states her sins are forgiven and that she can go in peace.

The Son of God, Jesus Himself in the flesh, received her worship and repentance and expressed forgiveness and the gift of peace. Jesus fully restored her.

But let us consider what happened in the days, months, and years to come. I have to imagine she was still triggered when she saw certain people or walked by certain places. I imagine she wrestled with grief over her choices or family circumstances, shame, and feelings of worthlessness. Perhaps her very home was the primary place she engaged in her sin and certain smells or items or experiences triggered flashbacks. I wonder when she felt comfortable to show up to church without worrying if leaders were going to look at her sideways. She was fully restored in that moment at Jesus' feet, yet the divine invitation is for Jesus to continue healing layers of her soul if she would allow Him to.

I recognize that I'm speculating a lot here. But these thoughts and questions are how we engage our faith with God. Too often we get stuck in binary thinking: "I sinned, so I'm bad." "I gave generously, so I'm good." "God heals on earth or in eternity."

We can each search our thought patterns to find more examples. But I find that life is so much more nuanced than the extremes that black-and-white thinking produces. In this case, viewing Heaven as a person who came to earth radically disrupts some of our traditional thoughts about Jesus.

We sin, and He redeems. We give generously, and we wrestle with stinginess. Jesus heals on earth—physically, spiritually, and mentally—and He heals in eternity. He can heal in mysterious ways, and He can heal through medication. Jesus can heal on earth in a moment, and He can heal on earth through process. We can observe and speculate about this process nature of God throughout the Bible in several examples.

Paul, who is famous for writing much of the New Testament, started in Scripture with the name Saul. He was a bounty hunter who searched for Christians to bring them to jail where many then faced execution. He was personally responsible as an accomplice and in voting for the murder of several Christ followers. He was radically saved with a post-ascension encounter with Jesus that literally knocked him into the dust of the earth and physically blinded him.[11] Jesus was seen through Saul's blindness. Saul's sight was restored and his spirit born again; he immediately became a preacher with a new name, Paul.

In the matter of a few days, he went from persecuting Christians to serving the early church, who worked to protect him from his old supervisors who plotted to kill him due to the change of his allegiance.

He was fully restored. Yet his memories were not erased. I can only imagine Paul traveling past the place Stephen was murdered in his own presence and approval. I can only imagine the grief and tears Paul held regarding the lives he participated in snuffing out. The families impacted. The impact those martyred lives could have had should they have continued. I can imagine the physical triggers of both witnessing and personally experiencing police brutality when Paul used to have been on the other end of it. I can imagine the shame spirals Paul engaged in. He was known as one who persecuted Christians.

I often find what we persecute externally is an overflow of all we persecute inwardly. When Paul's physical and spiritual eyes were opened, he was fully restored. Nothing more needed to happen. Yet, in God's loving kindness, I believe He beckoned Paul into continued layers of healing in his mind, emotions, and relationships.

Consider one of the closest disciples to Jesus, Peter. One of the most famous examples of restoration I can think of with Jesus is after Peter denies knowing Jesus three times in one night while Jesus was arrested and tried between Gethsemane and Calvary. After being denied by Peter three times, Jesus sits with him on the beach, roasting a fish breakfast. While Jesus prepares the meal, three times He asks if Peter loves Him. Three times with increasing emotional expression, Peter answers yes. A confession of love for each moment of betrayal.[12] Jesus didn't need to offer Peter this after the fulfillment of the cross and resurrection leading to salvation, yet He demonstrated care for the emotional restoration in the relationship, not strictly Peter's status of salvation.

In Jesus' famous Sermon on the Mount, He taught His followers a model for prayer. His model has since become the most recognized prayer in the world known by many traditions as "The Lord's Prayer." The structure of the prayer models honoring God as Father, submitting to God's will, and the human need to remind ourselves to trust in God's provision, leadership, and protection. This prayer is found in Matthew 6:9-13, and one line in particular stands out to me. Verse 10 says, *"Your kingdom come. Your will be done on earth as it is in heaven."* (NKJV)

I am sure this line has meant many things to many people. In the context of understanding Heaven, this part of the prayer feels more intentional than ever. Perhaps this prayer is preparing our hearts for the redeemed earth—that it will be what God always intended it to be. We know biblically that God's will in Heaven is for us to experience *complete* restoration. Yes, certainly God values spiritual wholeness and desires for us to experience this. He is spirit and made us in His image. And we have also seen how He has plans in Heaven for us to receive wholeness emotionally and physically as well. Jesus prayed that God's will would be done on earth, not just within the redemption of eternity. This example is clear evidence that Jesus—Heaven—cares about our *whole* restoration, not just our spiritual status alone. If this is His true longing as demonstrated with Peter, why would God withhold Himself until we reach eternity? "On earth as it is in Heaven" may very well be looking to the future of a new earth. But it may also be an invitation for Heaven to invade every part of our present earthly lives.

The Hebrew word for "earth" in Jesus' prayer can be translated as earth, land, or soil.[13] Dirt. The dust of the ground. What God fashioned human form from in Eden.[14] Was Jesus praying for God's will to be done within mankind, within you and I, just like it is in Heaven?

Genesis sets the precedent that we were made in His image.[15] Body, soul, and spirit. Male and female. I believe God's heart is for every part of our spirit, our physical body, and the soulish questions of identity, worth, and purpose to be fully healed and restored on earth as it is in Heaven. Perhaps there are some depths of pain that can only be redeemed in God's physical presence in eternity. However, what would life look like if we pursued layers of restoration in the here and now?

As a believer in Jesus, you are fully restored. You need nothing else You have an all-access pass to all of God and all of eternity.[16] Yet, more restoration is available to us if we engage with Jesus Himself. Layer by layer, like Peter, Paul, and so many others, He longs to heal and restore every broken, forgotten, lost, or wounded space in our hearts and minds. Engaging your story honestly with Jesus is the most important thing you can do to experience healing.

This kind of healing and restoration is not a checklist to complete. It is not going through a year of consistent counseling (though that's not a discouragement of the practice.) It is not something you achieve. It is a love you receive. A love none of us are worthy of. Yet Heaven Himself has reached out with human flesh to offer us this divine invitation.

The wounds of grief are layered and often so complicated due to their enmeshment with other areas of our heart and life. Heaven yearns to break into the overcast gloom grief has settled around you. What new layer of your heart can you open heavenwards?

GRIEF & RESTORATION

...RESTORATION IN GRIEF
IS LIVING A DUAL
REALITY THAT BOTH THE
PAIN IS AND WAS REAL.
AND THE RESTORATION
IS REAL AS WELL.
IT IS CARRYING BOTH
SORROW AND
GRATITUDE
SIMULTANEOUSLY.

CHAPTER NINE

THE OTHER SIDE

When we're fighting our way through the deepest, most daunting parts of grief, it's hard to picture the other side. Sometimes we even wonder if there *is* an "other" side. What if this is it? Treading wavy water without a life raft?

We've wrestled with the pain, with our origin and downfall, with the sin nature of the earth, with God's character, and with Heaven. Ideally, it has led us all to some hope for the other side. Now it's time to figure out that "other side," that future we hope for.

We have more biblical accounts of grief than many people recognize. The people of Israel as a whole experienced multiple layers of grief over hundreds of years. Grieving their sin; grieving being enslaved; grieving the invasion and destruction of their city, temple, and many cultural icons many times throughout history; grieving famine and devastation to the point of people dying of starvation; grieving their fellow countrymen, friends, and family members being captured or executed by invading nations.[1] The history of the people of God is not neat or simple. Even at the time of writing this book, we witnessed the largest terrorist attack on Jews in Israel since the Holocaust, and so the grief continues.[2]

After my father died, I read the whole book of Job. I have heard many a Christian walking through tragedy and adversity relating to some degree with the devastation Job faced. His life story exemplifies so many layers of grief with the additional challenge of everything the man lost happening back to back. Job experienced cumulative grief, which can often lead to complicated grief.

Cumulative grief is experiencing multiple losses in a short amount of time. Before you are able to process the loss, you experience another. If you have ever stood in the water near an oceanfront (or even the Great Lakes' beachfronts), you can perhaps imagine being unexpectedly knocked down by a wave. It can be very scary and is invariably uncomfortable (rip tides are no joke!). A large wave crashing into you causes disorientation, often involves salt going up your nose or into your eyes, and sand invades places you didn't invite. It can take a moment to catch your breath, get oriented, and assess the scrapes across your body from the sand and shells. Imagine trying to find your bearings, wiping the salty water that blurs your eyes, only to be taken out by another wave without you even seeing it coming. That is what cumulative grief feels like.

If you aren't familiar with the book of Job, it can incite both rage and comfort. Job is a generous, wealthy, God-fearing man who lives so uprightly, Satan asks God for permission to make Job's life miserable with the belief that if things got bad enough, Job would curse God. God grants the permission, specifying that Satan may not take Job's life. Satan runs with this and essentially causes every disaster possible to occur, some "natural" and some the result of enemies attacking and destroying or stealing. Job loses property, the lives of all his children, all his multiple kinds of livestock (which was his primary source of income), all his servants died except a handful who came to deliver the disastrous news from multiple directions, and to top it all off, Job falls ill to painful boils all over his body.

I see why Satan would think Job would curse God. The cumulative grief was overwhelming and deeply painful. Considering all of these mutual losses, Job's wife was not in the best of moods, so let's throw that into the mix of what Job is navigating. Job's three friends surround him and after a week of silence and mourning, the majority of the book is their speeches trying to figure out what is going on.

Job curses the day he was born, but never God. The friends believe Job must have sinned to deserve all the destruction with their belief that God would never permit suffering for nothing. As we already studied with Jesus in the New Testament, we can clearly see that pain, difficulty, and death on this earth are not the result of someone's personal sin but rather the sin-nature that the whole earth groans under the weight of.

The conversations among the four friends (Job and the other three) are irreverently honest. The questions we mull over in the midst of tragedy don't diminish us in God's eyes. We can ask questions, and we can feel big, wild feelings, yet not sin.

Finally, in the latter portion of the book, God begins to speak first with Job, then reprimand the friends for their false accusations about God's character. God gives a plan for restoration to the friends that includes Job praying for them. After forty-two chapters dialoguing pain, brokenness, excruciating grief, anger, questions, man's limited perspective, and God's character, we read about Job's restoration journey in the last eight verses of the book.

> *"After Job had prayed for his friends, the Lord restored his fortunes and gave him twice as much as he had before. All his brothers and sisters and everyone who had known him before came and ate with him in his house. They comforted and consoled him over all the trouble the Lord had brought on him, and each one gave him a piece of silver and a gold ring. The Lord blessed the latter part of Job's life more than the former part."* (Job 42:10-12, NIV)

The remaining verses inform how he received more sheep, camels, oxen, and donkeys than he had to begin with, and that Job even had ten more children.

Most grief support resources don't talk about the restoration part of the journey. We have plenty of resources of support, comfort, affirmation, and for feeling grief—especially while it is fresh or not fully processed. We need those resources, and I am grateful for them. But if we can conclude that there is hope in the grief journey, why does no one talk about restoration?

Many people view grief as a never-ending journey. Perhaps that depends on the definition of grief—whether it's the debilitating sadness and/or frustration often experienced in close succession to the event, or if it's any experience as a result of the loss. If there is no end to grieving, no end to the journey, then there can be no other side of grief. Some authors can shy away from the hope message because not every grieving heart is ready to embrace restoration at the same pace. It's actually a far more complicated conclusion, one that many people don't wish to live with. I believe restoration in grief is living a dual reality that both the pain is and was real, and the restoration is real as well. It is carrying both sorrow and gratitude simultaneously.

Picture Job holding his newborn child in the restoration season of his life. I can only imagine the joy, beauty, gratitude, and hope he held with that baby. And yet, it did not erase the sting from the death of his other children.

Humans have a difficult time with dual emotions—especially ones that seem opposing. It is almost as if giving into the joy of laughing along the grief journey can feel like a betrayal to the sadness or to the person we have lost. And likewise, holding onto the sorrow as we progress through life into more beautiful moments can feel like we are ignoring one or the other. How do you experience multiple complicated emotions all at once?

Many people are familiar with the term post-traumatic stress disorder, or PTSD. This is experienced by some in the wake of traumatic events of either high intensity like war, extreme conflict, or a debilitating medical issue, or of prolonged exposure of trauma like repeated abuse. Fewer people are familiar with the term PTG, or post-traumatic growth.

Richard Tedeschi, a professor of psychology who specializes in bereavement and trauma defines post-traumatic growth as "Positive psychological change experienced as the direct result of the struggle with highly challenging life circumstances."[3] It is not that the trauma or loss is good, but the platform of loss provides the opportunity for survivors to experience growth amidst wrestling with the pains of loss. Many people, though not all, report positive experiences and transformations despite difficult circumstances.

Resilience research continually indicates that acknowledging the full range of the emotional experience, giving space for both the highs and lows simultaneously, is how we process in order to move forward in health and growth. This is how we tenderly walk toward restoration.

I am fascinated by people who can restore old furniture or even take an old item and transform it into something different or better than it was. It is a type of creativity that I want to think I have, but I really don't. I can't naturally envision what it would look like to change a line of a chair or the fabric of a couch or the detail of a molding. I'm a very visual person, and it is hard for me to embrace what could be without being able to see it clearly and neatly laid out before me.

I suspect after the pain of loss, so many of us don't have the capacity to creatively envision what a restored life could even look like. But in my experience, restoration in the grief story is often subtle and reverent, not obnoxious and disorienting. It happens in the gentleness of healing one layer at a time which is in stark contrast to the harsh sweeping of our feet out from under us at the seashore.

Let's revisit the prophecy of Isaiah 61 that Jesus fulfilled. The third verse of this passage describes restoration following traditional Jewish mourning rituals.

Isaiah 61:3 (NIV): "to bestow on them a crown of beauty instead of ashes."

The word "ashes" in Hebrew symbolizes ruin, destruction, distress, sorrow, and humiliation.[4] Throughout the Old Testament, we read of God's people covering their head in ashes when in grief.[5]

Knowing God sees and honors our grief, I wonder if the crown of beauty is placed on top of the ashes—not in place *of* the ashes? That restoration with beauty in our life doesn't erase or "clean up" the grief, but rather shines over our grief? The crown of beauty represents restoration on the grief journey in our physical body.

Isaiah 61:3 (NIV): "the oil of joy instead of mourning."

In the resurrection passages, we read of several women going to the tomb as soon as they could after Sabbath to follow the Jewish custom in Jesus' time of anointing a dead body with spices and oil of myrrh to prepare the body for decay. This ritual was followed by all law-abiding Jews and served not only a practical purpose but also as an emotional ritual of finality and closure to face the reality of the necessity to mourn the death and loss.

Biblically we see oil represent anointing, a declaration made by someone with authority, and practical covering and protection.[6] God sees the oil we used in our grief (the kind the women brought to Jesus' body), *and* Jesus came to anoint us with a different kind of oil. The oil of joy represents restoration on the grief journey in our soul.

Isaiah 61:3 (NIV): "and a garment of praise instead of a spirit of despair."

The first time I was introduced to the concept of biblical restoration in grief was within the first year after my dad died. Mrs. Jones, who was no stranger to devastating loss, approached me and my mom at church. She expertly unclasped two gold bracelets off her arm, swiftly placing one on each of us. She made mention of the Old Testament and called the jewelry our "restoration bracelets."

It was a quick interaction and honestly, I was confused—especially since I was very much in the fog of grief brain (and as a teenager, I only wore silver jewelry—thank you very much). I didn't fully know what she was referring to, and I didn't understand the magnitude of generosity or symbolism attached to it, but I clung to it because she called it my restoration jewelry, and I found meaning in that. It was my garment of praise, and she was beautifully echoing how Job's community surrounded him in the restoration season.

Bracelets were a far cry from the other garments grievers wore in times past. In addition to the ashes, grievers in the Old Testament often wore sackcloth, an uncomfortable, itchy, humble garb. It visually alerted the community that the wearer was in a low place or depressed; they were denying their typical status of life financially and emotionally. Jesus restores us to cover ourselves in praise which (eventually) brings a greater measure of comfort than the depression of grief. The garment of praise represents restoration on the grief journey in our spirit.

When the Israelites were fleeing Egypt and walking into freedom after four hundred years of slavery, there are some crazy details to how it all went down. They carried unleavened bread (or flatbread) because they left Egypt so quickly, they didn't have time to add yeast, wait for it to rise, and prepare the bread in the usual fashion. We also read that the Israelites asked the Egyptians for their gold and silver jewelry, and the Egyptians gave it all to them, in addition to clothing![7]

To be sure, no amount of wealth justifies or compensates for that many centuries of slavery. Yet I can't help but see beauty in symbolism that the Israelites didn't just walk into freedom; they stepped into freedom dirty, bruised, rushed, cooking supplies on their back, scarred and blistered skin from working as slaves, with new clothing and restoration jewelry on. What a sight to picture them wandering the desert like this!

In fresh bereavement and in certain cases of grief, there is no capacity to think about your appearance. Just the basic hygiene routine can be a challenge, let alone thinking about how to coordinate an outfit and what jewelry to wear. And yet, even in that, it can almost be a symbol of rebellion to pain itself in caring for your body and adorning yourself with accessories. Today, my restoration bracelet still sits in my jewelry case among the few bracelets I own.

Some of my restoration stories I didn't even recognize until over a decade after my father's death. I often share with clients that I stepped into the space of grief counseling because of my own personal story. Walking alongside or sitting with someone in their grief journey is one way the ashes of my life have been covered in beauty. That my pain didn't end with me but produced an empathy to communicate with others sometimes without words.

Throughout my adolescence and young adult years, there were several men, similar in age to my father, who represented my dad to me in one way or another. It was so subtle, I couldn't notice it at the time. My dad was an optometrist yet knew a lot about the body. We rarely went to the doctor because Dr. Dad could diagnose and prescribe almost anything we needed.

After my dad passed away, God connected me with a Doctor Dad in our church. His presence, fatherly demeanor, well-timed humor, and freely shared wisdom has helped me navigate infertility, our young baby's variety of rashes, and so many other medical questions I would have gone to my dad for. Thank you, Doc.

Several men (and their wives) would provide "random" financial blessings either to my mom, to me as a college student, or by being first in line to dance with me at my wedding and slip a Benjamin in my hand. So many subtle little provisions that represented the covering and provision not just of an earthly father, but my heavenly Father, too. And then there was Sully.

Sully was a personal friend of my dad's. My dad introduced him to the adventure of serving on the foreign mission field, and Sully never let that go. He carried the mantle of missions in our church for decades after my dad died, and Sully was definitely a Missions Dad to many, including me. Sully was the most present and consistent father figure over the first decade of my fatherlessness. His irreverent humor and larger-than-life storytelling gave room for connection. He was there every Sunday at church, on all the mission trips encouraging my (and my future husband's) ministry gifts, at my high school graduation, and even filmed my wedding day. But it isn't the big moments that stand out. It was how he would text me any day that there was a cloudless sky and say he was praying for me. The little daily things are what impacted me. That's the influence a father has.

I know Sully has done that for so many other young people, not just me. But it truly impacted me in ways that I probably don't yet fully know. He kept sowing seeds into my heart, even when I didn't always receive or appreciate them. He is a picture of generosity with time, encouragement, consistency, and safe, fatherly love.

Do all these examples compensate for not dancing with my own dad at my wedding? For my Dad not composing a silly song for my young son, his grandson? Of course not. And yet, there is so much beauty in the gentle restoration of those examples and so many others.

I refer to the restoration process as gentle because it is slow and takes time. Again, it is a stark contrast to the whiplash of loss. Yet, restoration is not all sunshine and rainbows. Like many parallels of the physical healing process, restoration emotionally includes both healing and pain. Restoration has so much shade and color to it. It will mean different things to each one of us. Restoration can be in the form of a new job, new friendship, post-treatment life, accepting care, laughter, crucial conversations in repairing relationships, remarriage, learning to trust again, adopting a child, and the list goes on.

Each time you embrace the restoration, it forces you to acknowledge the loss. Every single time.

I'm so grateful for this new job, but man am I hurt over how I lost the last one.

I am so glad God has brought me new friendships to cultivate. But oh, the ache of acknowledging the drift in relationship with a friend who had previously been so close.

I am so excited to be pregnant again, but now I struggle with fear due to previous loss.

I'm overjoyed to be marrying again, but this joy stirs up pain from the past.

Every acknowledgement of the restoration forces you to face the dual emotions. It is gratitude and grief all at once. You wouldn't need the restoration had the loss not occurred. This makes restoration both exquisite and excruciating. This is how we continually acknowledge our grief without grief dictating our lives.

Just as grief is not linear, restoration is not either. We don't experience the joy of the Lord after our sorrows like marking a checklist.[8] Timothy Keller, a well respected theologian, shares, "The weeping drives you into the joy, it enhances the joy, and then the joy enables you to actually feel your grief without its sinking you."[9]

I don't believe we reach restoration at the finish line of grief. I believe we experience it along the long road of grief. And the more we step into it, the more we change and grow, often without realizing.

You don't have to "get" anywhere. Just keep gently stepping forward.

CHAPTER TEN

ALWAYS SHINING

Grief often reveals how we have taken things or people for granted. One of the most beautiful outcomes of walking through grief can be engaging with life more, telling people how you feel more (even in seemingly little ways), and living with fewer regrets. Even if it takes some time along your journey to get there.

One of the "brutiful" (brutal and beautiful) outcomes is that we realize life on this earth as we know it truly is short. This can cause us to live with urgency. There are many positive outcomes that can result from this, such as connecting more authentically within relationships, communicating more directly, being present to treasure time or special occasions, more boldly pursuing our purposes or passions, or doing fun or adventurous activities even when a little afraid or hesitant.

However, without healthy boundaries in our thought life, this urgency can give way to anxiety, and we can slip amidst the erosion of our internal peace. I was reflecting on this with a client as we discussed working through the fear of not having enough time. When our urgency turns into fear, we aren't living out of the optimal health available to us. There can be so much love in our sentiments and actions, but when love is wrapped in fear, the message gets lost. Holding onto love during grief processing is complicated.

I have personally walked through so many kinds of grief and bereavement that, in many ways, I feel strong and restored. And in many other ways, I am still navigating through measures of pain. As joyous as the restoration is, pain still is, and more grief and loss will be. It is so vulnerable to open your heart again after pain and loss only to eventually be met with more pain and loss. This is why so many hearts grow cold and calloused, numbing both the good and the bad. The fear of experiencing even more "bad" can be overwhelming.

And what happens when we have to grieve what we receive in the restoration? It almost seems cruel to live in the anointing of joy only to have to reapply the oil of mourning for what once was part of the restoration of joy. For example, what if Job had to bury one of his ten children from the restoration season of his life? What pain and questions would that have forced. The duality almost seems more than we can bear.

This is what I have been pondering over the past couple years of grieving pieces and people of my restoration story. In the summer of 2021, the delta variant of COVID-19 ravaged the Southeastern United States and caused more destruction in my personal world than any we had experienced in 2020. Our church experienced loss after loss, and we planned ten funerals in twelve weeks, most of which I had to livestream to limit exposure for myself and our young son. Crying and snotting into a paper mask is not preferable anyway.

Each loss affected me in one way or another—as a pastor, as a member of a community, as a friend, as someone who had already walked through *so. much. loss.* One funeral was for a mentor's mother. Kathy impacted me beyond my relationship with her daughter. Two funerals were for my friends' fathers. Watching two friends grieve their fathers due to tragedy, while also trying to be a pastor and leader and friend in their lives, was quite challenging and certainly triggered a lot of "I thought I was done with that" emotions. It was an impossible task because I wasn't just grieving witnessing my friends lose their fathers, I was also needing to personally grieve their fathers. Each man had brought fatherly love and godly encouragement to my life personally. They had each played a role in my restoration journey.

One, Sammy, was comfortable enough to tease me, was present to celebrate when my husband and I discovered the gender of our miracle baby, and later was the first person to treat our young son to experience an ice cream truck. Sammy asked our permission, of course, but only *after* our son was already sporting blue streaks of a melted Sonic head down his chin and arms as he happily smacked away at two green gumball eyes. I love that Sam knew the right "rules" to break as I imagine this is totally a move my dad would make as a grandpa.

The other was Sully.

What happens when we grieve one of our restoration relationships? At that point in my journey, I knew what to do to help myself grieve. I had all the tools and resources. I just didn't want to. I wasn't ready. I numbed my personal emotions and masked them under the strength of my pastor, leader, and friend hats. It is really easy to hide from grief when we want to, at least temporarily. We can lose ourselves in so much, both in healthy and harmful outlets.

When denying part of our reality, we look to escape our pain yet, we often end up perpetuating pain in the attempts to suppress it. Therapist and trauma survivor Aundi Kolber addresses this, "Certainly we do not want to make our home inside grief, but let us be clear: unless we make room for the reality of our entire human experience, grief will insist on taking over the whole house."[1] There are a lot of unknowns when we consider being honest about what we have tried to suppress. So amidst the shaky ground, we must look for firm footing with what we can know.

Once again, when grieving new layers of our life, we must come back to what we do know about God's character. Lamentations 3:33 (NIV) succinctly answers an element of God's heart that can be a balm of comfort and security to our souls: *"He does not willingly bring affliction or grief to anyone."* God was heartbroken with me, my friends, my church, and the world at large. That's the thing about healing and restoration. It isn't one and done.

As a child, I was a total tomboy and had my share of rambunctious adventures and personal injuries, including some tree falls complete with scrapes and splinters. If you have ever had a bad splinter, you know the pain your hot skin experiences as it is inflamed around the unwelcome intruder and does all it can to eject the invader. The grieving heart is much the same.

Like layers of skin pierced deep with a splinter, the heart and mind must heal one layer at a time. With each new layer of healing, a measure of relief and normalcy returns, yet there is still tenderness within the unhealed layers, whether we are looking at the wound or not. When we honestly engage our grief stories, we will discover new layers Jesus is inviting us to experience healing and freedom in. This is the "process" part of Jesus healing us on earth as it is in Heaven.

There are also ripple effects from loss in our lives that we only become aware of in time. This is partially because our brain can only handle so much processing at once, so we cannot grasp all the layers at once. This is also partly because we won't be aware of how the loss affects us until we engage new territory in our journey, and the echo of the loss becomes apparent to us. Just when I think I have mourned every element of losing my dad, eventually something new happens. I write my first book and can't share the process or my insecurities and joys with him.

A new ripple to wrestle with and grieve. A new loss to recognize from what was set into motion decades ago.

It is one thing to process a loss like losing a job. But in time, we face the ripples of losing the job, which leads to the loss of relationships with coworkers, financial security, routine, feeling competent or needed or purposeful, insurance, and even potentially the loss of community or a house if a new job opportunity requires moving. If we do not healthily engage our grief, there are even more complicated ripples.

Not addressing grief can cause anger, bitterness, or numb ambivalence to spill into our relationships or commitments. This can lead to secondary losses, like even more isolation and loneliness, friendships, a job, seasons of cold in faith or parenthood or marriage, or even divorce.

Despite the ripples and waves, I keep returning to the hope of Scripture, though. We must.

Make declarations like Psalm 71:14, 20-21 (NIV): *"As for me, I will always have hope; I will praise you more and more. Though you have made me see troubles, many and bitter, you will restore my life again; from the depths of the earth you will again bring me up. You will increase my honor and comfort me once more."*

Cling to promises from God like Joel 2:25 (NIV): *"I will repay you for the years the locusts have eaten."*

Like we've discussed previously, these declarations and this kind of biblical hope isn't just positive thinking. My husband wields a voice of enthusiastic hope. In contrast to him, I have often felt like I'm the "glass half-empty" spouse and have even joked that the only positive thing about me is my blood type!

But even though my natural perspective may not be instinctively and initially positive, I have learned how to live in hope. This is part of the dual reality we live in as believers on a fallen earth.

My dad was the king of Dad Jokes and, much like my husband, always had positive catch phrases. One of his phrases he would often use in the face of difficulty and darkness was, "The sun is always shining somewhere."

As a pilot, my dad had a unique perspective of weather and storms. There are two different sets of rules for piloting an aircraft: visual flight rules (VFR) and instrument flight rules (IFR). These rules dictate how a pilot navigates aircraft in various circumstances. Though I have never taken pilot lessons, I can imagine VFR would be much easier to navigate with quick confidence: I can see the runway is clear, so I'm landing. Simple.

However, IFR is required when the visuals are unclear, like in a cloud or storm. When conditions are overcast, a pilot cannot simply look out the window to know how to dodge traffic or turbulence. A pilot must learn how to rely on the instruments of the aircraft and the communication from the air traffic controller in order to know where to go, how to navigate a storm, or even where to land.

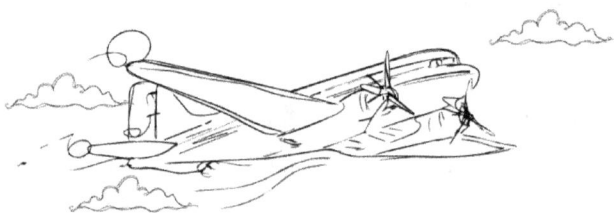

My first flight was at three weeks old in my dad's four-seater Cessna 172 Skyhawk. I was in full flight-attendant mode by eleven years old in our mission ministry's twenty-one-passenger taildragger DC-3, a World War II-era beauty. I don't remember taking a flight where I didn't personally know the pilot until after I could drive a car, and having to show up to an airport hours early was so weird to me. To this day, decades later, I still think it's silly to have to go to the airport early and will regularly be one of the last passengers to board a flight.

As a child, I got used to seeing the world from a higher elevation, with cars that crawled like ants as if the world itself was just a model landscape for a train set. I have a handful of good flight stories ranging from a turbulent lightning storm flying home from Haiti to a broken brake line in Honduras to the aircraft cargo door flying open while we were thousands of feet directly above the Gulf of Mexico.

One of my favorite flight memories, though, was flying back to the States from Spain. We took off from Barcelona in the late afternoon and flew westward. The unique timing led to us flying into the sunset for nearly six hours. I don't know if you're more of a sunrise or sunset kind of person, but the golden tangerine sky was hypnotic. It danced around our plane for five hours. The last hour, the sky painting ever-so-slowly progressed into a coral, fuchsia, and violet crescendo before eventually acquiescing into a pale twilight that guided the remaining few hours of our flight. I could not believe I witnessed a six-hour sunset. I have half a dozen photos of this sunset but of course, photos (not to mention the dirty airplane window) could never do it justice.

When your feet are on the earth, sunsets change so quickly and are rapidly fleeting. They're very easy to miss if you are indoors. When your feet are above earth, however, you see a different perspective. And if you had enough fuel, sunsets could be unending. When your feet are on earth, rainbows are splashed across the sky in a multicolored arc ranging from roughly forty-five to one hundred fifty degrees from the ground up into the clouds. When your feet are above earth, however, rainbows are a full 360-degree circle. Did you know that?

Our earthly perspective limits us to certain scientific wonders of our physical creation. Why would we think this limitation does not also apply to certain emotional and spiritual wonders? God's ways are higher than our ways. Much, much higher. Heaven has a higher, eternal view of our circumstances. Our limited view informs the posture of our grief. When processing loss, we naturally have an earth-centric view of loss. With all that we have explored about God's character and nature and all that we can know biblically about eternity, I invite you to expand your view to consider Heaven's perspective.

Pilots know that even if the sky is overcast, they simply have to increase elevation and break through the clouds in order to clearly see sunlight. This sometimes means purposefully flying into storm clouds and enduring turbulence and darkness to get *through* the storm and fly above it into sunshine once again.

"The sun is always shining somewhere." I never got the chance to ask my dad if he was actually saying "sun" or "Son," referring to Jesus. He would totally do something like that. But maybe he meant both.

In Heaven, Jesus is the source of light and provides practical, emotional, and spiritual illumination for everything we experience.[2] He stands above the clouds, and when we reach for Him, we will find Him. He is shining even now. Jesus already defeated sin by raising Himself from the dead,[3] yet as Randy Alcorn puts it, "the full scope of victory has not yet been manifested on Earth."[4] Jesus has done it, and He will do more when He returns to earth. He is life and He will destroy death.[5]

After Jesus returns, *"no longer will there be any curse"* (Revelation 22:3, NIV). We will, once again, taste the full restoration of Eden. As hard as I try, I don't know that I can picture sensory paradise, let alone complete emotional paradise and utter spiritual freedom. This will be a glorious day. And yet, I know we are still very much in the present. And if you find yourself in a storm of grief presently, I weep with you.

The storms and losses that have happened in your life are not perfection. Death is not good. Yet, we know God is still good. He can work all things together for our good even out of something that is so not good.[6] God is still good, even when we cannot see or feel Him all the time.

For pilots to fly above gloomy weather, IFR certification is required. You can fly relying on your visuals if things are clear thousands of feet above you and miles around you. However, when life gets stormy, you have to learn to rely on what the instruments tell you, and what the control tower communicates to you in order to navigate the gloom. The instruments give indications of what is going on immediately around the aircraft.

The air traffic controller gives insight into the whole orchestration of the hundreds of aircraft in the region.

You weren't meant to navigate the journey of grief on your own. There are tools to guide you, people who are certified, and the voice of the Spirit longing to guide you. The thing about flying with instruments? The path is charted out before the aircraft ever takes off. Every decision a pilot will make has already been approved by the air traffic controller. The pilot simply has to follow the course and the instructions. The pilot never needs to hesitate to ask permission to enter certain airspace or hesitate if a particular route is the best path.

Though life isn't ever as easy as to go on auto-pilot, there is a simplicity and freedom in sticking to the course and the instructions given to you. Someone else already did the work to plot the trip, account for ever-changing weather, and calculate the load you'd be hauling. I believe God invites us into this via His Spirit, His people, and resources we are surrounded with.

Second Corinthians 13:9-11 (NIV) encourages us to strive for full restoration. To me, this language implies many settle for partial restoration, partial healing, and partial joy. I have witnessed people attempt to pursue restoration for themselves in their own strength. This leads to partial restoration. I have witnessed people search for restoration outside of God. This leads to a long, empty, relentless search.

When the disciples were being tossed about their ship in a merciless storm, and they feared for their lives, in desperation they cried out to wake Jesus from His sleep to save them.[7] This word "save" from New Testament Greek is sōzō and it also appears in Romans 10:9, which states, *"If you declare with your mouth, 'Jesus is Lord,' and believe in your heart that God raised him from the dead, you will be saved"* (NIV). The same word is used in the context of being saved from this life of sin we were born into as well as being saved from the life storm around us. Sōzō means salvation, but it also means safe and means to be made whole.[8] Whole. Complete. Nothing missing. Nothing broken.

My stubbornness may be partly DNA and partly what my trauma story forged in me, but if I know there is an option for full restoration, I'll always dig my heels in and fight for that. It isn't easy along the way, but it is worth it every time. The same invitation is available for you.

Some storms take us by surprise. Others we can see brewing on the horizon. Some storms clear quickly. Others are excruciatingly long. Storms pass and sunshine returns. And our need to navigate more storms in the future is guaranteed. We aren't responsible to stop the storm or to understand it. We cannot make it go away, and we cannot protect those we love from experiencing their own storms. We are responsible for moving through the storm, navigating above the dark clouds to get back to the light.

The gloom and fog of grief can paralyze us in the storms of loss. Knowing God's heart and truth helps us stand firm in trust so we can gently pursue complete healing. And though we may not be able to see the radiance or feel the warmth all the time, the Son is still shining. Always shining.

THANK YOU

As an independently published book, your rating and review helps others find this book. If this book impacted you, please rate and review it on Amazon and Goodreads.

Review on Goodreads

Review on Amazon

APPENDIX

While not everyone who navigates grief experiences clinical depression or is at risk for suicide, this topic is one that comes up frequently in both the church and grief spaces. Both those in active grief and those who love the bereaved may desire clarity and greater understanding of what a typical grief experience with depression looks like. This appendix is a more expansive conversation on the topic from Chapter Three.

As mentioned previously, situational depression and clinical depression can exist at the same time but are different. Recognizing the differences can be a crucial step in seeking the appropriate help and support.

Situational depression often occurs after life-altering events, such as the loss of a loved one and includes many of the typical symptoms seen in bereavement as noted in Chapter Three. Conversely, with clinical depression, such as Major Depressive Disorder or Seasonal Affective Disorder, there are some distinct differences that grief would not typically introduce. In grief, pain typically comes in waves interspersed with happy memories of the deceased or the way circumstances used to be. In clinical depression, mood and interest are mostly decreased for more than two weeks at a time without much variation. In grief, self-esteem is typically maintained, whereas in clinical depression, self-loathing and feelings of worthlessness are common.

In bereavement, desires of wanting to be with your loved one are common, although plans to actually end one's life are not. In clinical depression, desires or thoughts to harm self or take one's own life arise from feelings of worthlessness, feelings of being undeserving to be alive, and feelings of overwhelm not being able to navigate the depression.[1]

Psychiatrists describe the brain circuitry as being out of balance during depression, particularly with below normal activity, which impairs the abilities to focus and concentrate, plan, organize, problem-solve, and manage life stress.[2] Sleep deprivation first impacts this same part of our brain as well. Another part of the brain that is underactive in depression contributes to ambivalence and emotional distance from things and people. This gives language for why people experiencing depression often cannot make up their minds and have little capacity to engage in empathy. As much as there are parts of the brain underactive during depression, there are other parts that are overworking.

During depression, the amygdala, the brain's alarm and fear alert center, is overactive. This produces a hormonal cocktail keeping the brain on alert for threats with a sense of fear, dread, uneasiness, and/or impending doom. Conversely the brain's pleasure center is unresponsive when depressed. It is clear to see how this contrast would be terrifying—to be constantly on alert and feeling a sense of inadequacy, fear, cloudy thoughts, emotional muting and distance from others, trouble making decisions and unable to problem solve all while objectively good things are unable to be felt.[3]

As we discovered with Dr. Jennings' work earlier, this damage occurring within the brain is not strictly emotional or psychological. As the body is continually in this stress cycle, it activates the immune system to be on high alert, and inflammation occurs throughout the brain and body, which causes damage to otherwise healthy cells, tissue, and even organs. Though each case is unique in its intricacies, this is a reminder that caring for our mental health impacts our physical health.

One important reminder is that clinical depression is treatable! Holistic approaches provide the best outcomes.

If you or a loved one are experiencing symptoms of depression, please reach out for help. Licensed mental health therapists or psychiatrists are excellent sources to begin with. If you are in more immediate need of assistance, please call the Suicide and Crisis Lifeline. Call or text 9-8-8 anytime 24/7 in the United States to connect with someone to speak to in both English and Spanish. If you are located outside the United States, please call your local emergency number or suicide hotline number. You don't have to walk alone.

NOTES

INTRODUCTION
[1] 2 Corinthians 2:4 (ESV).

CHAPTER ONE | SENSELESS
[1] Genesis 1:10-25.
[2] v. 31, emphasis added.
[3] Genesis 2:16-17.
[4] Genesis 2:17.
[5] Genesis 3:21. Note: there is mystery here regarding what "garments of skins" means exactly. Does it mean God killed an animal for this clothing project? Does it mean God created skins since He had just created everything in the universe as we know it? Do the skins come from an animal or were the humans somehow living without human skin prior to sin? This topic, among others, is part of a longstanding debate between different theological schools of thought, particularly regarding if God wields the power of death or if God is the source of life and that Christ's sacrifice on the cross was to "destroy him who had the power of death, that is, the devil" (Hebrews 2:14, NJKV).
[6] Genesis 3:4-5.
[7] Romans 6:23.
[8] Genesis 3:16-19.
[9] Andrew Newberg, M.D. and Mark Robert Waldman, *How God Changes Your Brain: Breakthrough Findings from a Leading Neuroscientist* (Ballantine Books, 2009).
[10] "Daily meditation on a God of love for one month produced reductions in heart rate, blood pressure, and stress

hormone levels as well as a 30% increase in memory testing."
Tim Jennings, M.D., "How TV and an Angry, Wrathful God
Damage Your Brain," *Come and Reason Ministries*. January 28,
2021,   https://comeandreason.com/how-tv-and-an-angry-
wrathful-god-damage-your-brain.

[11] Tim Jennings, M.D., *The God-Shaped Brain: How Changing
Your View of God Transforms Your Life* (InterVarsity Press,
2017), 27–32, 53.

[12] Jennings, "How TV."

[13] Jennings, *God-Shaped Brain,* chap. 4.

CHAPTER TWO | RUNNING IN SAND

[1] Psalm 78:58; 2 Corinthians 11:2.

[2] Psalm 78:58; Matthew 21:12-13; John 11:33; Isaiah 63:10.

[3] Genesis 2:23, 25; 3:6.

[4] Any time we try to fill in the blanks for someone else, we
almost always get it wrong.

[5] Genesis 32:26 (NIV).

[6] Genesis 32:28 (NIV).

[7] For many stories I share in this book I have changed names
or details to protect the privacy of those involved. The
individuals whose journeys I describe have been given the
opportunity to review and approve of the way their stories
have been presented. Some requested actual names to be used
as a way to honor someone who has finished their life on this
earth or to honor how they themselves have overcome storms
in life.

[8] Deuteronomy 31:6; Hebrews 13:5.

[9] Daniel 3:17-18a (NIV).

[10] Tim Jennings, M.D., email to author, July 29, 2023.

[11] William W. Seeley, "The Salience Network: A Neural
System for Perceiving and Responding to Homeostatic
Demands," *Journal of Neuroscience* 39 , no. 50 (2019): 9878–82,
https://doi.org/10.1523/jneurosci.1138-17.2019.

¹² Billy Graham, "The Healer of Our Broken Hearts," *Billy Graham Evangelistic Association.* July 9, 2004, https://billygraham.org/story/the-healer-of-our-broken-hearts/.
¹³ Romans 8:15; Matthew 7:11.

CHAPTER THREE | WHY?

¹ Genesis 2:17 (NIV).
² Judges 6:13 (ESV).
³ Ruth 1.
⁴ 1 Samuel 1.
⁵ Psalm 10 and Psalm 13, to name a few.
⁶ Luke 2:48.
⁷ Luke 2:49.
⁸ Matthew 27:46; Mark 15:34; emphasis added.
⁹ Isaiah 53:5; Hebrews 4:15.
¹⁰ Psalm 139:14.
¹¹ Psalms 42:11; 43:5 (NIV).
¹² Romans 12:2; Proverbs 4:23; Colossians 3:2; Philippians 4:8.
¹³ See *Your Brain is Always Listening* by Dr. Daniel Amen for more on this topic.
¹⁴ Golia Shafiei, Yashar Zeighami, Crystal A. Clark, Jennifer T. Coull, Atsuko Nagano-Saito, Marco Leyton, Alain Dagher and Bratislav Mišić, "Dopamine Signaling Modulates the Stability and Integration of Intrinsic Brain Networks," *Cerebral Cortex* 29, no. 1 (2019): 397–409, https://doi.org/10.1093/cercor/bhy264.
¹⁵ "Dopamine," Cleveland Clinic, accessed 2024, https://my.clevelandclinic.org/health/articles/22581-dopamine.
¹⁶ See *You, Happier* by Dr. Daniel Amen for more on this topic.
¹⁷ The Suicide and Crisis Lifeline is 9-8-8, which is available 24/7 in the USA via call or text. They will connect you with someone to speak with in both English and Spanish.

CHAPTER FOUR | LOST & FOUND

[1] C.S. Lewis, *A Grief Observed* (Hassell Street Press, 2021), chap. 2.

[2] John Piper, "What's the Difference Between Faith and Hope?," *Desiring God*, August 19, 2022, https://www.desiringgod.org/interviews/whats-the-difference-between-faith-and-hope.

[3] 100 Humans, "Pain vs. Pleasure" *Netflix* video, 41:00, March 13, 2020, https://www.netflix.com/title/80215997?source=imdb.

[4] Carla J. Berg, C.R. Snyder, and Nancy Hamilton, "The Effectiveness of a Hope Intervention in Coping With Cold Pressor Pain," *Journal of Health Psychology* 13, no. 6 (2008): 804–9, https://doi.org/ 10.1177/1359105308093864.

[5] 1 Samuel 16:7.

[6] John 17:12.

[7] Tim Jennings, M.D., "Suicide and the Myth of Lost Salvation," *Come and Reason Ministries,* December 3, 2017, https://comeandreason.com/suicide-and-the-myth-of-lost-salvation/.

CHAPTER FIVE | BE STILL & KNOW

[1] Psalm 46:10 (NIV).

[2] Kenneth E. Bailey, *Jesus Through Middle Eastern Eyes* (InterVarsity Press, 2009), 193.

[3] John 11:21, 32.

[4] John 11:37 (ESV).

[5] Jeremiah 33:3.

[6] "Shiva and Other Mourning Observances," Chabad-Lubavitch Media Center, https://www.chabad.org/library/article_cdo/aid/291135/jewish/Shiva-and-Other-Mourning-Observances.htm.

[7] Psalm 34:8, Psalm 103:13; Matthew 7:9-11; Luke 18:19.

SECTION THREE | GRIEF & HEAVEN

1 Often referred to as Jesus' second coming.

2 Often referred to as Jesus' millennial reign.

3 *Heaven* by Randy Alcorn (www.epm.org); *In Light of Eternity* by Randy Alcorn (www.epm.org); Magazine: *The Wedding of Christ to His Bride* by Dr. Timothy Jennings, *The Case for Heaven* by Lee Strobel.

CHAPTER SIX | HEAVEN IS A PLACE

1 Genesis 1:20; Deuteronomy 26:15; 1 Kings 22:19; Matthew 6:9; Matthew 28:2; Luke 2:15; John 14:2.

2 Hebrews 12:23.

3 Randy Alcorn, *In Light of Eternity* (WaterBrook, 2009), 41.

4 John 14:2-3.

5 Hebrews 11:10, 11:16, and 13:14; Revelation 21:2.

6 Hebrews 8:5 and 9:24; Revelation 5:8, 8:6, and 15:2.

7 Revelation 5:9-14.

8 Revelation 21:4-5.

9 1 Corinthians 15:54; 2 Corinthians 5:2-3; 2 Timothy 4:8; James 1:12; 1 Peter 5:4; Revelation 2:10; Revelation 6:11.

10 Luke 22:29-30.

11 Esther 1-10.

12 Revelation 6:9.

13 Ephesians 3:15; Revelation 5:9-12; Revelation 6:10.

14 Luke 6:21.

15 2 Kings 2:11; Isaiah 11:6-8; Isaiah 63:25; Revelation 8:13; Revelation 19:14.

16 Genesis 3:17-19.

17 Isaiah 65:23; 2 Timothy 2:12; Revelation 22:3, 5.

18 Isaiah 65:21; Ezekiel 47:9-10.

19 Revelation 21:19-21.

20 Isaiah 11:9; 1 Corinthians 13:9-12.

21 Revelation 14:13.

22 Revelation 22:2.

23 Revelation 20:4-6.

[24] Revelation 6:10.

[25] C.S. Lewis, *The Problem of Pain* (Harper Collins, 2015).

CHAPTER SEVEN | HEAVEN IS A HEALING

[1] Matthew 17:20 and John 13:13-14.

[2] 1 Corinthians 15:40-51.

[3] Genesis 18, Joshua 5, and Daniel 3.

[4] Genesis 3:8.

[5] John 1:14.

[6] 1 Corinthians 6:19

[7] Jennie Lusko, *The Fight to Flourish: Engaging in the Struggle to Cultivate the Life You Were Born to Live* (Thomas Nelson, 2021).

[8] Blue Letter Bible, "Strong's H3368 – Yāqār," https://www.blueletterbible.org/lexicon/h3368/kjv/wlc/0-1/.

[9] Randy Alcorn, *Heaven* (Tyndale House Publishers, 2011), 462.

[10] "Exodus 15:26," Names of God in the Old Testament, Blue Letter Bible, https://www.blueletterbible.org/study/misc/name_god.cfm.

[11] Matthew 9:29; 10:52; and John 9:6-7.

[12] Luke 17:14.

[13] Matthew 8:3 and Mark 1:41.

[14] Mark 5:27-28.

[15] Acts 3:6-7.

[16] Hebrews 13:8.

[17] John 11:14-15, 41-42.

[18] Matthew 5:45.

[19] Genesis 3:1

CHAPTER EIGHT | HEAVEN IS A PERSON

[1] Leviticus 16.

[2] Randy Alcorn, *In Light of Eternity* (WaterBrook, 2009), chap. 7.

[3] John 11:11-14.

4 Acts 7:60.

5 Jennings, *God-Shaped Brain,* chap. 4.

6 John 10:10.

7 2 Timothy 1:10 and 1 John 3:8.

8 John 19:30.

9 2 Kings 5.

10 Luke 5.

11 Acts 9.

12 John 21:15-17.

13 Blue Letter Bible, "Strong's G1093 – Gē," https://www.blueletterbible.org/lexicon/g1093/kjv/tr/0-1/.

14 Genesis 2:7.

15 Genesis 1:27.

16 Matthew 16:19 and Romans 8:14-17.

CHAPTER NINE | THE OTHER SIDE

1 See the Old Testament books of Ezra, Nehemiah, Isaiah, Jeremiah, Lamentations, Ezekiel, Daniel, and Hosea for the variety of examples listed.

2 October 7, 2023, by the terrorist organization Hamas.

3 Richard Tedeschi and Lawrence Calhoun, "Posttraumatic Growth," *Encyclopedia of Mental Health (Second Edition),* 305–7. https://doi.org/ 10.1016/B978-0-12-397045-9.00246-9.

4 Blue Letter Bible, " Strong's H665 - 'Ēpēr," https://www.blueletterbible.org/lexicon/h665/kjv/wlc/0-1/.

5 2 Samuel 13:9; Esther 4:1; Daniel 9:3; Jonah 3:6.

6 1 Samuel 16:13.

7 Exodus 12:34-36 (NIV) and Exodus 32.

8 Nehemiah 8:10.

9 Timothy Keller, *Walking with God Through Pain and Suffering* (Penguin Books, 2015).

CHAPTER TEN | ALWAYS SHINING

[1] Aundi Kolber, *Strong Like Water* (Tyndale House Publishers, 2023), chap. 2.

[2] Revelation 21:23 and 22:5.

[3] Hebrews 2:14.

[4] Alcorn, *Heaven*, 103.

[5] John 14:6 and 1 Corinthians 15:25-26.

[6] See Romans 8:28.

[7] Matthew 8:24-25.

[8] Blue Letter Bible, "Strong's G4982 – Sōzō," https://www.blueletterbible.org/lexicon/g4982/kjv/tr/0-1/.

APPENDIX

[1] Chinenye Onyemaechi, MD, ed. 2024. "What Is Depression?," *American Psychiatric Association*, April 2024, https://www.psychiatry.org/patients-families/depression/what-is-depression.

[2] Daniel G. Amen, *You, Happier* (Tyndale Refresh, 2022).

[3] Jennings, *God-Shaped Brain*.

ABOUT THE AUTHOR

Connoisseur of oat milk lattes, aspiring 3.5 pickle ball player, and sore loser of board games, Amanda McNeil holds a BA in Psychology from Southeastern University and attended Heritage University and Seminary for both her MA in Christian Counseling and Doctorate in Psychology and Theology. She is a Temperament Counselor and Licensed Pastoral Counselor with the NCCA and holds over a decade of experience. She is a Certified SYMBIS Facilitator for premarital counseling. She was ordained as a Pastor in 2012 at City of Life Church in Orlando, FL, where she currently serves as an Executive Pastor.

As a young person, Amanda experienced family tragedy and learned how to draw near to God in the middle of it. This inspired her drive to help others find hope in the darkest of seasons. She is also passionate about helping marriages thrive with healthy communication, continued intimacy, and balancing budgets, parenthood, and goals. She has facilitated premarital counseling for hundreds of couples over the last fourteen years.

Amanda, her husband, Justin, and their miracle son are Florida natives. Overcoming the dynamics of being raised in a blended home, personal tragedy, grief, and facing infertility, have given her an authoritative voice of hope.

She is the author of *Grief Journal*, available in both English and Spanish, and the co-author of *Meant to Be: A Devotional for Husbands and Wives*.

CONNECT WITH
AMANDA

amandacmcneil

amandacmcneil.com

www.ingramcontent.com/pod-product-compliance
Lightning Source LLC
Chambersburg PA
CBHW050651270326

41927CB00012B/2976